SCREENING THE NOVEL

SCREENING THE NOVEL

REDISCOVERED AMERICAN FICTION IN FILM

GABRIEL MILLER

with photographs

FREDERICK UNGAR PUBLISHING CO. / NEW YORK

*for Kathy
and in memory of her father*

Printed in the United States of America

LIBRARY OF CONGRESS CATALOGING IN PUBLICATION DATA
Miller, Gabriel, 1948–
    Screening the novel.
    Bibliography: p.
    Includes index.
    1. American fiction—Film and adaptations—
Addresses, essays, lectures.   I. Title.
PN1997.85.M5   813'.54'09   79–48071
ISBN 0–8044–2622–8

Design by Marsha Picker

ACKNOWLEDGMENTS

First, Stan Hochman, my editor, whose idea this book was, and whose many valuable suggestions have helped along the way. Very special thanks to Allen Estrin at Films Incorporated, who was more than generous in helping me to view some of these films, and to Dan Wickenden at Harcourt Brace Jovanovich, who provided material on Edward Lewis Wallant. Eternal gratitude to Pat McCarney, the world's greatest typist, for shaping up the manuscript in record time despite an unintelligible draft, and to Barry Levy, for all those talks about films and directors over too much coffee and whatever at the Third Avenue El, and mostly to Kathy, whose patience and tolerance have been tested on every chapter.

CONTENTS

INTRODUCTION

This book contains examinations of eight neglected American novels and the films made from them. To be sure, some of the works included here might not seem to have been entirely "neglected"—*The Postman Always Rings Twice*, for instance, has enjoyed a wide international readership—but until quite recently, none of these novels has received much scholarly attention, nor have their writers yet gained sufficient acknowledgment among critics and students of literature. Quite recently, some of these novelists have begun to attract the notice they deserve, and I hope that the discussion of them here will stimulate further critical interest.

As the preceding remarks indicate, my choices of material for this book were dictated by the novels and their authors rather than by the film adaptations. The films, for the most part, were well received and commercially successful; in some cases they were responsible for whatever popularity the source novels have enjoyed. The relative obscurity of the originals may, indeed, have contributed to this success, as the films have thus escaped the burden of comparison imposed by the critical preconceptions often brought to the viewing of a film based on an accepted literary masterpiece. Having no acquaintance with the novel, the critic or viewer could approach the film as an independent work of art, unconcerned with its comparative value as an adaptation.

Such comparative analysis is, on the other hand, the basic method in this study, which has been undertaken for the purposes both of judging the respective merits of each novel and film complement and of discovering some more general tendencies and techniques of the adaptation procedure itself. The relative unfamiliarity of these selected novels, again, may have authorized a considerable latitude for revision in the process of transposition from the printed page to the screen, thereby supplying vivid evidence of the differing characteristics of the two media. In examining these works, then, it is possible to observe and classify certain common practices of the adapter's art, as well as to observe the success of some individual efforts of novelists, directors and screenwriters.

In most cases, the filmmakers have reduced or simplified the scope of the novels they were adapting. For example, devices such as subplots have been either eliminated or much curtailed, usually to the film's advantage—in the cases of *The Pawnbroker* (1961), *Susan Lenox* (1931), and *Paths of Glory* (1957), various secondary story threads have been eliminated in order to give the films smoother plot lines. This streamlining process has the added advantage of focusing and accentuating the development of one or two central figures, a concentration of story interest that facilitates the fast pace and visual mode of film narrative. An example of insufficient streamlining can be found in *The Gangster* (1947; *Low Company*), in which too many peripheral characters were kept in and left undeveloped, considerably weakening the narrative thrust of the film—apparently one of the dangers of a writer's adapting his own work is an inability to let go of some of his creations.

The makers of two films based on very short novels, *They Shoot Horses, Don't They?* (1969) and *Hester Street* (1975; *Yekl*), have attempted to expand the scope of the books, with differing results. Sidney Pollack, director of *They Shoot Horses*, gets trapped in the dilemma of remaining faithful to the novel's spirit while realizing the necessity of altering its design, and as a result never really manages to free his film from the strictures of its fictional world. Joan Micklin Silver, on the other hand, succeeds in recreating Abraham Cahan's fictional universe in *Hester Street* by opening up its social environment, while even altering his thematic focus as well—the concerns of her film are less rooted in Cahan's 1890s than in the wider, timeless values of traditional social comedy.

The richness and complexity that language can convey through symbol and metaphor, as has been pointed out by many critics, is not often handled well in film. In fashioning *The Gangster*, Daniel Fuchs and Gordon Wiles wisely eliminated much of the symbolic quality of *Low Company*, where, as in any successful novel, the characters grow out of the language patterns used to portray their thoughts and words. In the film much of this verbal portraiture (unfortunately, not all of it) has been replaced with a series of conventional figures and patterns of the gangster film genre.

Director Stanley Kubrick, indeed, was able to supply his own powerful visual metaphors, sometimes even eliminating the need for dialogue at all, in creating his film version of Humphry Cobb's generally unmetaphoric novel, *Paths of Glory*.

The films considered here generally have different thematic objectives than their fictional counterparts. A filmmaker may depart almost entirely from the design and tone of the source work, as in *Hester Street,* wherein Silver has transformed an essentially closed and claustrophobic novel into an open and vibrant film narrative. The time lapse between the two creations is surely significant in such a case—Silver's film appeared some seventy years after Cahan's novel.

More often, a novelist's personal, corrosive vision is merely softened by the filmmaker. Many of the books considered here have a closed, restrictive design, and the world view presented tends to be pessimistic, dominated by despair or at best tinged with sadness. Their screen versions are usually more optimistic: the film of *The Postman Always Rings Twice* (1946) ends on a strange religious note which is quite alien to Cain's nature; John Huston tones down B. Traven's cynicism in *The Treasure of the Sierra Madre* (1948); and Stanley Kubrick's ending of *Paths of Glory* cushions the audience from the violence and the finality of Cobb's conclusion. David Graham Phillips' biting exposé of the victimization of women by the industrial society of turn-of-the-century America in his novel *Susan Lenox* becomes in Robert Z. Leonard's hands a sudsy Hollywood romance about the triumph of true love. *The Gangster,* although it concludes with the death of its protagonist (who does not die in the novel), ends more positively than *Low Company,* for Shubunka's death in the film is one of choice and even defiance, raising him to a heroic stature that the character totally lacks in the novel.

Only the films of *The Pawnbroker* and *They Shoot Horses* remain true to the spirit of their originals, though in the case of the latter, McCoy's narrative has been so tampered with that his dramatic ending does not seem to have been earned in the film version. *The Pawnbroker,* on the other hand, is itself an exception to the general rule of pessimism among these novels, for Wallant's protagonist actually moves toward a final measure of redemption. The film follows the same pattern, echoing the novel's tone of muted, guarded optimism, as in both cases, the ending has been achieved at the price of extreme suffering and death.

The novels' characters undergo a simplification process when transferred to the screen, for film is not very successful in dealing either with complex psychological states or with dream or memory, nor can it render thought. As George Bluestone points out, in *Novels into Film:*

> The film, by arranging external signs for our visual perception, or by presenting us with dialogue, can lead us to infer thought. But it cannot show us thought directly. It can show us characters thinking, feeling, and speaking, but it cannot show us their thoughts and feelings. A film is not thought; it is perceived.

As a result, certain dimensions of a fictional character must be eliminated in portraying him/her on the screen. John Huston's three prospectors in *Treasure* seem less in conflict with themselves and more with each other than in the novel. Sol Nazerman in the film *The Pawnbroker* appears more single-mindedly indifferent than his counterpart in the novel, where Wallant dramatizes more of his home life, especially his sympathetic relationship with his nephew; in the film, also, Nazerman's memories of the past must be introduced in connection with various confrontations he has during the day, while in the novel they (more naturally) haunt his dreams. Stanley Kubrick's Colonel Dax in *Paths of Glory* becomes an exemplary figure of bravery and integrity rather than the more human soldier plagued by doubts and fears, presented in Cobb's novel.

As a medium that most successfully accommodates realism, film is equally unsuited to the portrayal of grotesque or symbolic characters. Daniel Fuchs' monstrous Shubunka is thus humanized in the film, while also made stronger and more attractive. Gloria of *They Shoot Horses, Don't They?*, who really lacks human dimension, but functions as a symbol of existential isolation and despair in McCoy's short novel, becomes more vulnerable, sympathetic and three-dimensional in the film.

Such metamorphoses spring primarily from the nature of the medium itself. Fiction achieves a greater density because of its length—the experience of reading most novels is longer than that of viewing most films, and the reader can control his own exposure to the material, interrupting his reading, referring back, or skipping ahead—while most films are limited to about two hours' running time, and the film audience's experience is bound, to a large extent, by the speed of the projector, which allows no breaks (except for the rare intermission), and no opportunities to review what happened earlier. The film must make its point and deal with its characters and subject quickly and directly, in a basically linear sequence of images. Writers and directors must recognize and try to work within these simple and seemingly obvious guidelines in order to achieve a successful transformation of the novelist's art into the language of the cinema.

Only two of the directors considered here have yet attracted significant critical attention—Stanley Kubrick and John Huston (though few of Huston's films have been subjected to close analysis). Both men, interestingly enough, have based much of their work on novels, often "important" novels. Sidney Lumet, who is beginning to receive more attention, developed his early career almost entirely through adaptations (Reginald Rose's *Twelve Angry Men*, Tennessee Williams' *The Fugitive Kind*, Arthur Miller's *A View from the Bridge*, Eugene O'Neill's *A Long Day's Journey into Night*) and has more recently directed such films as Chekhov's *The Seagull, Last of the Mobile Hot-shots* (Tennessee Williams' *The Seven Descents of Myrtle*), and Peter Shaffer's *Equus*.

Studies of adaptation such as this should function as a kind of corrective to the auteur theory. Most American directors do not write their own original scripts, and although a director may make changes in the nature of a novel or play he/she is adapting and in certain ways stamp the film with his/her own personality, the source of the film's basic ideas and vision is generally contained in the novel or play. Indeed, some less successful adaptations fail in part because the director/writer cannot find a happy medium between the novelist's vision and his own.

I expect that there may be some surprise occasioned by my choice of material for this book—everyone surely has his own candidates for rediscovery. Certainly there are a number of works I regret not including here—Willard Motley's *Knock on Any Door,* Wallace Markfield's *To an Early Grave (Bye, Bye, Braverman),* Edward Anderson's *Thieves Like Us,* Alvah Bessie's *The Symbol (The Sex Symbol)*—the list is long, and obviously everything could not be included. I opted for longer essays about fewer book/film pairs over shorter chapters and more subjects and aimed for an interesting cross-section of periods and styles. In general, I have selected authors whose careers (comprising more than one noteworthy novel) I consider worth rediscovering, my hope being that the essays on these particular novels and films may encourage readers/viewers to look more closely not only at the novels and the films but into the careers of the writers (and in some cases, the directors) as well.

GABRIEL MILLER

1

JEWS
WITHOUT MANNERS

THE NOVEL
Yekl: A Tale of the New York Ghetto
(1896, Abraham Cahan)

THE FILM
Hester Street
(1975, Joan Micklin Silver)

Joan Micklin Silver made her feature film directorial debut with an adaptation of a novel buried in the obscure recesses of American literary history—Abraham Cahan's *Yekl: A Tale of the New York Ghetto,* the first novel of a Jewish Russian immigrant who came to America at the age of twenty-two, unable to speak English. Its subject matter, the Jewish immigrant's problems in adapting to America at the turn of the century, was hardly a burning issue in 1975. Cahan himself devoted much of his life to making the acculteration process easier for immigrant Jews, and, consequently, much of his novel's topical urgency has become merely interesting lore of a bygone era for the contemporary reader. However, by altering the narrative tone, the character focus, and the generic structure of this work, and revising somewhat its thematic emphasis, Silver managed to transform *Yekl* into a vibrant, amusing study of manners and morals in transition— in effect translating Cahan's period piece into the timeless language of comedy, which embraces both the old and the new worlds.

Abraham Cahan was the first important American-Jewish writer. When one looks at his life and work, however, his literary career must take a back seat to what was Cahan's life work—the Yiddish newspaper *The Jewish Daily Forward,* which he helped found, and of which he was the senior editor for nearly fifty years. His career as a writer of fiction occupied considerably less of his time: it began in 1891 with the publication of his first Yiddish story, "Mottke Arbel and His Romance," and ended abruptly with his most famous novel and his masterpiece, *The Rise of David Levinksy* in 1917, written in English.

Cahan, one of the most influential journalists of his time, was born in 1860 in a small village in Vilna, Lithuania, a town known for its learning and intellectual life. A descendant of rabbis and the son of a teacher, Cahan naturally spent his youth in reading and study, attending various Hebrew schools and Yeshivas. He began to drift away from religion, however, when he enrolled in a Russian Jewish school that offered secular courses. Later he received a teacher's license, joined a literary circle, and then definitely abandoned Judaism to become a Socialist. When, after the assassination of Alexander II by an anarchist group, the government began to repress political activity, Cahan decided to leave the country. In 1882 he illegally crossed the border to Austria and later that year arrived in the United States.

He quickly became part of the radical community of New York's Lower East Side, immersing himself in American politics, labor activities, and the study of English. Soon he was writing pieces for various papers, notably *The Workman's Advocate* and the organ of the Yiddish-speaking Socialists, *The Arbeiter Tseitung;* for four years he was a reporter on *The*

Commercial Advertiser, edited by Lincoln Steffens. Cahan's political-journalistic activities culminated in 1897 in the founding of *The Jewish Daily Forward*, which he took over as editor in 1903. Though Socialist in ideology, this paper was primarily committed to the acculturation of the largely immigrant Jewish population. Acting as a kind of father figure and teacher to an uneducated community, editor Cahan gave his people a paper that was easy to read and filled it with features like "Bintel Brief" (A Bundle of Letters), a popular column which answered questions of all kinds and provided advice on subjects ranging from table manners to politics. Thus the *Forward* sought to bring its readership into closer touch with the new land; by 1924 it was reaching a quarter of a million readers.

Even while engrossed in political causes and newspapers, Cahan was also beginning a career as a man of letters. His first short stories in English, "A Providential Match" and "A Sweatshop Romance," appeared in *Short Story* magazine in 1895. By the following year, he had become a serious literary figure, with the publication of his first novel, *Yekl: A Tale of the New York Ghetto*.[1] Interestingly, William Dean Howells, the most influential critic of his age, was directly responsible for the writing of *Yekl*. Impressed by the story "A Providential Match," he sent for Cahan, talked with him, and encouraged him to do a more substantial piece on ghetto life. Cahan set to work on the novel immediately, soon completed it, and sent it to Howells, who praised the book with the judgment that "an important force had been added to American literature." Dissatisfied with the original title, *Yankele the Yankee*, it was he who suggested that Cahan change it to *Yekl: A Tale of the New York Ghetto*.

Finding a publisher was difficult. Many turned it down, claiming, like the editor of *Harper's Weekly*, that "the life of an East Side Jew wouldn't interest an American reader." Finally, Howells succeeded in placing it with Appleton Crofts and then reviewed it himself in the *New York World*:

I cannot help thinking that we have in him a writer of foreign birth who will do honor to American letters. . . . He is already thoroughly naturalized to our point of view; he sees things with American eyes, and he brings in aid of his vision the far and rich perception of his Hebraic race; while he is strictly of the great and true Russian principles in literary art. . . . Yekl is in fact a charming book.[2]

As a writer of fiction, Cahan labeled himself a realist. In an essay published in *The Workman's Advocate* in 1889, he wrote that the concern of literature should be in faithfully presenting "the thrill of truth." He singled out Tolstoy as the greatest of the realists and later praised Howells. As a Socialist, Cahan felt that, ultimately, realistic art and socialist politics must work toward the same goals.

In *Yekl* he began developing the major themes of his best fiction—the spiritual dislocation caused by the Jewish immigrants' exposure to American life and the resulting feelings of loneliness and emptiness. At the end of his best novel *The Rise of David Levinsky,* David, who came from a Russian *shtetl* to become a millionaire in America, ultimately mourns the disintegration of his spirit in words that echo a widespread feeling of loss:

. . . I cannot escape from my old self. My past and my present do not comport well. David, a poor lad swinging over a Talmud volume at the preachers synagogue, seems to have more in common with my inner identity than David Levinsky, the well known cloak-manufacturer.[3]

Cahan's achievement as the preeminent novelist of the Jewish immigrant experience sprang from his ability to discern the contradictions inherent in the two very different lives the immigrant knew. His fiction dramatizes the difficulty of achieving the successful transition that Crèvecoeur foresaw for the new man who could leave behind "all his ancient prejudices and manners" to adopt "new ones" from the new way of life he had embraced. Cahan knew, and his characters must learn, that often this achievement may be bought only at the cost of the individual soul, and his stories regularly focus on this loss of the self and on the failure of love that may accompany it.

Yekl's protagonist, Jake Podgorny (Yankl in the old country), has been in America for three years, during which time he has completely discarded his old world values (adherence to traditional Judaism) while trying to become "a regalah Yankee." He prides himself on how Americanized he has become: "Once I live in America, I want to know that I live in America. Dot'sh a' kin' a man I am!"⁴ The greatest shame is to be a "greenhorn" (the name given to immigrants, newly arrived, who retain their old world appearance), and Jake has done everything to *oyshgreen* (Yiddish for "cease to be green") himself—changed his name, cut off his beard, and begun to wear fancy clothes. While most of the serious-minded workers in the New York cloak factory where he is employed devote their free time to study, Jake spends his in trying to impress everyone with his knowledge of such "Yankee" pastimes as boxing and baseball. Cahan, however, manages to undercut this boasting, emphasizing in dialogue the comic grotesquerie of his overzealous attempts to adopt the American manner:

> . . . "Jimmie Corbett leaked him, and Jimmie leaked Cholly Meetchel, too. You can betch you' bootsh! Johnnie could not leak Chollie, becaush he is a big bluffer, Chollie is. . . . But Jimmie pundished him. . . . He tzettled him in three roynds." (p. 2)

Neither his fellow workers nor the women he takes to a local dancing academy know that Jake has a wife and son in the old country waiting to be sent for. The pleasures of his new life have dulled his desire to bring them over, and despite occasional pangs of conscience, he keeps putting off sending them the money for their passage. Then one day he learns in a letter that his father has died, and, at last overcome with guilt, he decides to send for his wife, Gitel, and his son, Yossele.

When Gitel arrives, Jake is dismayed by her old-fashioned, pious appearance. He immediately loses patience with her "greenness," and, despite Gitel's attempts to modernize herself, the chasm between them grows. Meanwhile Jake becomes increasingly involved with Mamie, a flashy "Americanized" woman he has met at the dancing academy. When he learns that Mamie has saved up a considerable amount of money, he agrees to use it to secure a divorce from Gitel. The story concludes as Gitel and Bernstein, Jake's pious, gentle and scholarly roommate, are planning to marry and open a grocery store, while Jake and Mamie are riding the trolley to City Hall to get married. Jake views his future with mixed feelings, however, belatedly considering the prospect of life with the shrewish Mamie. At the novel's end he is reluctant to have the trolley car reach its destination.

Cahan develops his themes primarily by focusing on the consciousness of Jake (Yekl), who is basically a shallow man, rather vulgar and morally weak. Totally preoccupied with appearances and surfaces, he is contrasted in the opening scenes with his more serious co-workers who demonstrate the old world values of learning and a deeper kind of self-improvement. It is Jake's careless rejection of these values, which at first makes him merely ridiculous, that will eventually lead to his more serious and permanent loss of dignity. The point is made clear when Bernstein, who later boards in Jake's house, teases him about his interest in "childish things," for Jake responds to his changing world as a child does, innocently delighted by its superficial pleasures and irresponsibly ignorant of its deeper meanings.

This weakness of character accounts, in part, for Jake's ultimate failure to make good his pretensions, but Cahan insists that America itself must share the blame. No sentimentalist, Cahan does not advocate old world Judaism over American modernity, but he feels strongly the need to strike a balance between the divergent values of the two societies. The important intellectual and communal values fostered by Judaism are threatened by the highly individualistic, materialistic, and often shallow life style of capitalistic America, though that same new world spirit must be applauded for its power to free the immigrant of many of the illiberal, superstitious elements of the old doctrine, as well as the stifling control of the ghetto. Successful transition to the new life, Cahan implies, requires a deliberate and thoughtful choice of the best of each of these worlds, a creative blending of past and present. In Jake, he presents a character who has swallowed America whole and rejected the past completely, without giving either one much thought. The novel's portrayal of this man's progress from euphoric pursuit of American style to a final sense of loss reflects the tragic possibilities of the immigrant's failure to harmonize the two worlds of his experience.

Jake is yet not able to forget the past completely; thoughts of his life in the old country occasionally recur to him, but, handicapped by his pride and by a basic inability to think things through, he cannot manage to integrate them with his new life:

> . . . his Russian past appeared to him a dream and his wife and child, together with his former self, fellow characters in a charming tale, which he was neither willing to banish from his memory nor able to reconcile with the actualities of the American present. . . . He wished he could both import his family and continue his present mode of life. (p. 26)

The news of his father's death inspires him to a powerful, though temporary, resolve:

> Ah, if he could return to his old home and old days, and have his father recite the sanctification again, and sit by his side opposite

his mother. . . . "I will begin a new life!" he vowed to himself. (pp. 30-31)

Such a "new" life, however, is beyond his reach, for he has already lost contact with his past and so can no longer achieve the balance of old and new that might allow him both success and happiness. Under the influence of guilt and grief, he does send for his wife and child, but the rest of the tale must demonstrate how the American experience has burned his better half away.

Gitel, too, confronts the conflict between the traditional past and the progressive modern spirit of the new land. Her inability to forsake the old and embrace the new with Jake's enthusiasm precipitates their break-up, for she is, in fact, a living, breathing example of everything he has tried to leave behind. It is her appearance that eventually becomes the central, symbolic issue in their divergence of values: like any *shtetl* woman, Gitel dresses simply and wears a *shaitel* or wig (religious law required that Jewish women shave their heads at marriage and thereafter keep them covered with a wig or kerchief). When Jake objects that this is not the fashion in America, she wants to please him but is torn by her loyalty to the old world tradition. In a revealing private moment, Cahan details the elements of Gitel's dilemma:

> Now, however, as she thus sat in solitude, with his harsh voice ringing in her ears and his icy look before her, a feeling of suspicion darkened her soul. . . . "He must hate me! A pain upon me!" she concluded with a fallen heart. . . . At one moment she took a firm resolve to pluck up courage and cast away the kerchief and wig; but at the next she reflected that God would be sure to punish her for the terrible sin, so that instead of winning Jake's love the change would increase his hatred for her. (p. 42)

Like Jake, she is unable, at this point, to make an intelligent compromise between old and new.

Hester Street: Gitel (Carol Kane) confronts physical and emotional isolation in the new land.

A central scene in the novel involves Gitel's confrontation with Mamie, the "dance hall girl" who will eventually lure Jake away from her. Mamie is everything Gitel is not—in her seven years in America she has taught herself to speak English, but, more importantly, she is a student of fashion. Again, clothes are symbolic of the wearer's cultural loyalties, and Mamie is decked out in the brilliant colors of the American flag:

> She was apparently dressed for some occasion of state, for she was powdered and straight-laced and resplendent in a waist of blazing red, gaudily trimmed, and with puff sleeves, each wider than the vast expanse of white straw, surmounted with a whole forest of ostrich feathers, which adorned her head. One of her gloved hands held the huge hoop-shaped yellowish handle of a blue parasol. (pp. 48-49)

Gitel "instinctively scented an enemy in the visitor," recognizing in her a personal rival for Jake's affections as well as the dazzling embodiment of the new world style that she herself lacks. Inspired to compete with this Yankee siren, she makes some tentative adjustments in her own appearance, but it is too late—Jake, by now thoroughly infatuated with the modern Mamie, has no more patience with his wife's conservative ideas and cannot be won back by such partial measures.

Their relationship continues to deteriorate until finally he can resist no longer, but goes to Mamie and declares his love. This episode, which takes place on the roof of Mamie's apartment building, skillfully combines the central elements of Cahan's theme:

> When they reached the top of the house they found it overhung with rows of half-dried linen, held together with wooden clothespins and trembling to the fresh autumn breeze. . . . A lurid, exceedingly uncanny sort of idyl it was; and in the midst of it there was something extremely weird and gruesome in those stretches of wavering, fitfully silvered white, to Jake's overtaxed

mind vaguely suggesting the burial clothes of the inmates of a Jewish graveyard. (p. 75)

The scene has a quality at once comic and macabre, for in declaring his love to Mamie, Jake knows that he is cutting himself off permanently from the past, and his anxieties take shape, grotesquely, in the billowing linen: ". . . while she was speaking his attention had been attracted to a loosened pillowcase ominously fluttering and flapping a yard or two off. The figure of his dead father, attired in burial linen, uprose to his mind" (p. 77).

Jake is moving, however, awkwardly and confusedly, into a new realm of experience, the modern mode of life that underlies the facade of Yankee stylishness—divorce, unheard of in the old country, will swiftly follow upon the love affair, which is equally alien in traditional experience. As Jules Chametsky points out, "the new imperfectly assimilated language could not in the mouths and hearts of these immigrants achieve mature fidelity,"[5] and Cahan is able to reflect the clumsy progress of the lover's feelings by exploiting the comic, yet touching vulgarity of the dialogue as Jake and Mamie confront the possibility of his divorce:

> "Dot's all right," she returned, musingly. "But how are you going to get rid of her? You von't go back on me, vill you?" she asked in English.
> "Me? May I not be able to get away from this spot. Can it be that you still distrust me?"
> "Swear!"
> "How else shall I swear?"
> "By your father, peace upon him."
> "May my father as surely have a bright paradise," he said, with a show of alacrity, his mind fixed on the loosened pillowcase. "Vell, are you *shatichfied* now?" (p. 79)

Rendered inarticulate in the face of a complex reality, they plunge on into a new world of manners and of morality, accompanied by persistent pangs of guilt in memory of the past that is being left behind.

The difficult details at last worked out, Jake gets his divorce, Mamie gets Jake in exchange for some of the money she has saved since coming to America, and the novel ends, ironically, with Gitel triumphant. She will use the money to open a grocery business and marry Bernstein, who has not been completely tainted by American values and so can still appreciate a woman such as Gitel. Her experiences with Jake have taught her something of the world:

> The rustic, "greenhornlike" expression was completely gone from her face and manner . . . and . . . there was noticeable about her a suggestion of that peculiar air of self-confidence with which a few months' life in America is sure to stamp the looks and bearing of every immigrant. (p. 83)

Gitel thus has begun to assimilate some of the American ways, but her upcoming marriage to Bernstein hints at a determination to hold on to the old world values that she knows and respects. Apparently capable of achieving the creative balance of old and new, she faces a future of bright prospect.

Jake, on the other hand, is a "defeated victor." Mamie has trapped him, and he quickly begins to feel his loss:

> He was painfully reluctant to part with his long-coveted freedom so soon after it had at last been attained, and before he had time to relish it. . . . Still worse than his thirst for a taste of liberty was a feeling which was now gaining upon him, that instead of a conqueror, he had emerged from the rabbi's house the victim of an ignominious defeat. (p. 89)

He is the first significant protagonist in Cahan's fiction to be defeated by the new land—it is clear here that America, adopted irresponsibly and hastily, as Jake adopts it, is a dangerous source of a corruption. (Later, in *The Rise of David Levinsky*, Cahan would return to this theme, to elaborate with rare artistry upon the tragedy of the immigrant experience.) In Jake's story he exemplifies, with some humor, the hazards involved in the sudden transformation to a new way of life:

> During the three years since he had set foot on the soil, where a "shister [Yiddish for shoemaker] becomes a mister and a mister a shister," he had lived so much more than three years—so much more, in fact, than in all the twenty-two years of his previous life—that his Russian past appeared to him a dream and his wife and child, together with his former self, fellow characters in a charming tale, which he was neither willing to banish from his memory nor able to reconcile with the actualities of the American present. (pp. 25-26)

Failing to attain such reconciliation, this man must suffer the pain of a fractured personality and the thwarting of all his hopes of freedom and glamor.

Yekl lends itself readily to the transposition to film because of the photographic realism of many of its scenes and its broad simplicity of characterization. Cahan's tale is brought vividly to life in *Hester Street,* though characters and themes have been somewhat altered in the transition. The most radical difference is one of tone, for the film aims rather at the human comedy of the immigrants' social predicament than at the serious consequences of their cultural dilemma.

Whereas the character of Jake clearly dominates the novel, appearing in nearly every scene and carrying the thematic burden of the story, Joan Micklin Silver's film concentrates instead on the contrasting energies in Jake's social world. In order to bring the world of the Lower East Side at the turn of the century into sharper focus, subordinate characters are more fully developed: Bernstein, Mamie, Mrs. Kavarsky (a friend of Jake's), and Joe, the owner of the dancing academy, all have prominent roles in the film.[6] Gitel (Carol Kane), to whom Cahan devotes few scenes, becomes almost as important as Jake (Stephen Keats) in the film's action, and the part of Yossele/Joey, their son, is much magnified in order to further humanize the family.

Silver's decision to develop characters gives the film a stronger narrative line than the novel, but achieves it at the expense of thematic power. Many of the emotional and spiritual difficulties encountered in adjusting to America are touched on, but the contradictions of faith and hope they involve are never fully explored. A whole new emphasis is created by the film's dual focus: whereas Cahan concentrates on his theme, at the expense of plot, by focusing entirely on Jake, Silver wants to highlight, as well, the Americanization of Gitel, and the divided narrative that results tends to undermine the significance of the cultural dialogue which gives the novel its meaning.

In both versions Jake is presented as a loud, boorish fellow obsessed with acquiring the American manner, but Cahan develops, in addition, a spiritual dimension in his character by revealing Jake's thoughts and feelings throughout the action. Obviously conscious of the comparative weakness of her medium in dealing with such psychological complexity, Silver prefers to treat the conflict of styles in sharper contrast by transferring this spiritual quality to the character of Bernstein (Mel Howard), the studious factory worker who eventually marries Gitel. Quiet, patient, and scholarly, Bernstein, however, does not become a sympathetic enough character to make it clear that Jake has really given up anything substantial in becoming a "Yankee." He is kind to Gitel when Jake ignores her, he tries to make excuses for Jake's inattention, and he teaches Joey the *Aleph Beth* (alphabet), but ultimately he is supposed to seem admirable because of what he is not (Jake) rather than because of what he is. This representative of the old world virtues too obviously lacks any qualities that would enable him to succeed in the new world, and the film's ending suggests that is it Gitel's developing modernism rather than any of the traditional Jewish values he exemplifies that will govern his chances of happiness in the future.

Mamie (Dorrie Kavanaugh), too, quickly becomes an important figure in Silver's version, for the film opens at the dancing academy, where she sees Jake, rather than at the cloak factory, where Jake and Bernstein work. The love affair plot receives further emphasis in the next scene, as Mamie, Jake and Joe discuss love in America, Jake insisting that "in America you marry for love, dats all." Following this, Jake and Mamie are seen flirting in the lobby of her apartment house. Indeed, the lovers are shown together much more often in the film, flirting and even kissing passionately, and their mutual attraction has already been made clear before the rooftop scene, which is the high point of the novel. *Hester Street*'s Jake and Mamie belong to a much livelier social world than Cahan could, or would, depict, and rather than stumbling along clumsily toward a declaration of their love, they by now have only to plan the necessary divorce.

Unlike Cahan's, Silver's women are rather good at the game of love, and even Jake displays a certain flair for romance that he lacks in the novel. Where Cahan dwelt upon his characters' comic inability to express feelings of love, the film instead shows them practicing artful wiles and stratagems in the romantic struggle. Mamie, of course, is an accomplished modern flirt, and Gitel, also, despite her old-fashioned appearance, soon learns to seek out her man. Too late and too slow to win back the infatuated Jake, she attracts and snares his timid friend with a sure instinct. Silver invents a family picnic scene in the country wherein Gitel flatters Bernstein's scholarly bent and defends him against Jake's teasing, and later, when Jake has gone and the divorce is pending, she all but proposes to Bernstein herself. Self-directed and intelligent in the rise of their feminine powers, these women (and also Mrs. Kavarsky, who advises Gitel in her troubles), are much more actively involved in shaping their own lives than was allowed by Cahan, whose pre-feminist mentality spared them little sympathy.

Silver's contemporary sensibility is most apparent in her treatment of Gitel, who is a far stronger and more attractive character in the film than in the novel. When she removes her wig and dresses up to prove to Jake that she is adjusting to America in order to win back his love, the adjustment here (unlike in the novel) makes a real difference—she is suddenly more attractive—and if Jake's angry reaction in pulling at her hair is thus made puzzling, Gitel's effort at least is admirable. Again, when Jake finally leaves her, the Gitel of the novel is distraught; in the film she is calm, even unemotional. Next Silver shows her shrewdly bargaining for all of Mamie's savings in a legal settlement that precedes the divorce—the scene has no basis in *Yekl*—and she remains composed throughout the divorce proceedings, which Silver details at length, whereas her counterpart in the novel simply fainted.

This Gitel is an admirably independent and resilient individual who recovers from the culture shock embodied in Jake's rejection by learning to adapt to American ways, and so she requires none of the pity that Cahan's Gitel must inspire. After the divorce ceremony, the rabbi's wife asks the name of the boy, and when Mrs. Kavarsky (Doris Roberts) answers "Yossele," Gitel corrects her, saying, "No, Joey," thus making clear her recognition of the need to make some concessions to the new land. She herself may remain emotionally tied to the old world manner, as her marriage to Bernstein implies, but she is now frankly determined that her son, at least, will be freely exposed to the American culture.

Thus investing much new strength in the character of the deserted wife, *Hester Street* provides a dual portrait of the immigrant experience, focused on the ironic pattern of role-reversal that underlies the story.

As the film ends, Jake and Mamie are walking to city hall to get married, unable to afford a ride—in the novel they take the trolley—because Gitel has gotten all of Mamie's money. Their plan to start a dancing academy is likewise thwarted, and Jake already has the air of a henpecked husband: once a fast-talking, flashy dresser who exulted in the freedom and the glamor of the American style, this unfortunate has traded in the old country wife he could master for a modern woman who will thoroughly dominate him. In order to emphasize the contrast in the prospects of the two new couples, Silver also brings together in her closing shot Gitel and Bernstein, who are discussing their planned grocery business. Matching Mamie in the decisiveness of her control, the newly emancipated Gitel insists that she will run the store, leaving Bernstein free to study. Tactfully appealing to his judgment, however, in a deft gesture of traditional wifely deference, she asks if he thinks they should sell soda and seltzer, and the camera withdraws on a humorous note as Bernstein, ever the discursive Talmudist, replies: "In hot weather people are thirsty—on the other hand such items can be bought on the streets as well . . . so we mustn't be too quick to say dis or dat."

Silver's comic ending epitomizes the mood of detached amusement with which she views the immigrant experience in America. Some eighty years removed from the conflict of cultures, she cannot treat the story of Jake Podgorny with the conviction of tragic loss that pervades Cahan's novel. Perhaps Jake is, after all, too shallow, too simple a character to call up the sympathy an earlier generation might instinctively have felt for a man in his situation. In any case, he and Gitel and Mamie and Bernstein now emerge as slightly ridiculous, and rather endearing, figures engaged in a comic dance of changing partners.

Silver's style emphasizes her comic detachment, openly and freely playing over the scene of the drama. Looking in on a world that she never experienced, her camera seems to be discovering and exploring it rather than creating it. In a marvelous sequence when Jake takes Joey out to see America for the first time, the viewer is invited to experience, from the child's perspective, the variety, excitement, and the noise of the crowded streets. The sense of exhilaration, thus inspired, of new worlds beyond the experience of the immigrant in the *shtetl*, of possibilities suddenly opened up, infuses the film with a joyous tone that is diametrically opposed to the claustrophobic vision conveyed in Cahan's depiction of this same street life:

> He had to pick and nudge his way through dense swarms of bedraggled half-naked humanity; past garbage barrels rearing their overflowing contents in sickening piles, and lining the streets in malicious suggestion of rows and trees. . . . The pent-in sultry atmosphere was laden with nausea and pierced with a discordant and, as it were, plaintive buzz. (p. 13)

Yekl's immigrants, and particularly its protagonist, exist in an oppressive environment of urgent tensions, deceptive appearances, and the threat of tragic failure. Silver's characters, clearly, inhabit another world—open, energetic, and promising—and theirs is a story of the struggle to cope with its mysteries, told with some affection and much humor. Its closing image is provided by a high-angle shot of the two couples discussing their futures as they leave the frame in separate directions, entering a larger world of renewed hopes and extended possibilities that lie beyond.

Raymond Durgnat has written that "film's job is not so much to provide information about the characters' minds as to communicate their experience."[7] *Hester Street* is an extraordinary document of a certain group's "experience" and a very good example of how an imaginative director can reshape and redefine a work of fiction to suit the dynamic visual priorities of the film medium.

2

THE NEW WOMAN
GETS THE
OLD TREATMENT

THE NOVEL
Susan Lenox: Her Fall and Rise
(1917, David Graham Phillips)

THE FILM
Susan Lenox: Her Fall and Rise
(1931, Robert Z. Leonard)

David Graham Phillips' novel *Susan Lenox: Her Fall and Rise* contains all the ingredients for an exciting film—its beautiful and spirited heroine develops a variety of relationships with a number of men, among them a newspaper reporter, a distinguished playwright, and a gangster, and her adventures on the road to a final brilliant success involve a series of dramatic settings, including a riverboat which houses an acting company, the slums and piecework factories of turn-of-the-century New York City, the underworld of prostitution and corrupt politics, the glamorous society of Paris and London, and the world of theater. Phillips himself zealously makes the most of his sensational material, enhancing its natural appeal with his strong sense of photographic detail, realistic locale, and vivid dialogue. The creators of the film version, unfortunately, chose to disregard this gift package Phillips had provided them, and ended up making use only of his title and a number of (much revised) plot details. His serious thematic exploration of the social and personal effects of poverty, women's rights, and the excesses of capitalism is reduced in the film to an uninteresting tale of the torturous road true love must follow in pursuit of a happy ending. *Susan Lenox* is remarkable as the only film in which Greta Garbo and Clark Gable starred together—the "irresistible force met the immoveable object," but instead of realizing the obvious, strong potential of this pairing, director Robert Z. Leonard managed a film that has neither force, vitality, nor intelligent content.

David Graham Phillips' own life would have made for a fairly interesting Hollywood scenario as well: he was born in 1867 in Madison, Indiana, an Ohio River town, to solid, religious, middle-class parents. He left home after high school to matriculate at nearby Asbury (now DePauw) University, but soon left for Princeton, where he exhibited a certain literary bent and graduated in 1887. Through some friendships made at Princeton, Phillips secured a job as a reporter for the Cincinnati *Times-Star*. Talented enough to be lured away by the rival *Commercial Gazette* at a higher salary, he built a considerable reputation with his feature and gossip columns, and even became a local celebrity, "the star reporter of the town."[1]

In 1890 Phillips hit the big time, joining the staff of Charles A. Dana's New York *Sun*, meanwhile beginning to contribute fiction and essays to *Harpers Weekly*. His reformist tendencies were developing, however, and three years later he left the *Sun* to work for Joseph Pulitzer on the New York *World*. Here he served variously as a reporter and commentator on the New York scene and as the paper's London correspondent. By 1896 he had become Pulitzer's expert on European politics, and was soon contributing regularly to the editorial page. It was on the *World* that Phillips first began applying in earnest the "muckraking" abilities that would later bring him into yet greater prominence.

Because of his professional association with the *World*, he published his first novel, *The Great God Success* (1901), under the pseudonym David Graham, before leaving the paper the following year to devote himself to this, what he considered more serious, kind of writing. During the next nine years he would produce more than twenty novels, most of them attacking business or political corruption, among them *The Cost* (1904), a novel dealing with Wall Street, *The Plum Tree* (1905), a novel about political corruption, and *The Deluge* (1905), which dealt with trusts.

In 1906 Phillips achieved a great deal of notoriety when William Randolph Hearst's *Cosmopolitan* published the first in a series of articles, entitled "The Treason of the Senate," which Phillips wrote to expose various U.S. senators' involvement in graft and subservience to the demands of big business:

> A scorching and unsparing spotlight, directed by the masterly hand of Mr. Phillips, will be turned upon each of the iniquitous figures that walk the Senate stage at the national Capitol. This convincing story of revelation . . . is a . . . terrible arraignment of those who, sitting in the seats of the mighty Washington, have betrayed the public to that cruel and vicious Spirit of Mammon which has come to dominate the nation. . . . Who is to protect us from the Senate? . . . Who, then is to protect the people but the press?[2]

It was this series which prompted President Theodore Roosevelt to label Phillips "the man with the muck-rake." Although these articles received some high praise in reformist circles, Phillips was also subjected to a great deal of abuse, not only from the president and government officials, but from the press as well—he was condemned as a sensationalist and an opportunist, and his articles were criticized as poorly researched and presented.

Deeply disturbed by this treatment, he resolved anew to remove himself from journalism and devote his energies entirely to fiction. Becoming interested in the concept of the "New Woman," he now devoted his attention frequently to the subject of marriage and to the problems women face in breaking into and succeeding in the male-dominated business world. His best-known work in this vein, and perhaps the finest novel he ever wrote, was *Susan Lenox,* published in two volumes in 1917. Phillips worked harder and longer on this novel than on any other—having begun it in 1904, he continued revising and polishing it until his death in 1911.

He did not live to see his masterpiece published, nor the four other novels that were on his desk—he once remarked that "if I were to die tomorrow, I would be six years ahead of the game."[3] On January 23, 1911, leaving his Gramercy Park apartment on the way to the nearby Princeton Club, he was shot by Fitzhugh Coyle Goldsborough, a disturbed violinist who believed that his family was being attacked in Phillips' novels and that his sister had been libelled in a recent Phillips novel, *The Fashionable Adventures of Joshua Craig* (1909). The absurdly melodramatic tenor of this episode reached its height when, after shooting Phillips, Goldsborough committed suicide; Phillips died in Bellevue Hospital the following day.

Susan Lenox grew out of Phillips' muckraking impulses. As a New York journalist concentrating on the exploration of crime and vice, he became interested in the plight of the single woman who, if unable to deal with work in the sweatshops, was often forced into prostitution. Scandals involving prostitution, especially organized rings which included police and politicians, were beginning to attract big press in the late 1890s, as a rise in prostitution was facilitated by the passage of the 1896 Raines Law, which permitted New York saloons to sell liquor on Sunday if they operated in conjunction with a hotel (at least ten beds). Magazines and newspapers published articles and stories about the young women who fell prey to unscrupulous recruiters (known as "cadets"), madames, and "protectors." O. Henry's famous tale, "An Unfinished Story," dealt with this subject, as did Reginald Kauffman's *The House of Bondage*, which went through sixteen printings within a year of its publication in 1911.

Phillips' heroine, unlike O. Henry's or Kauffman's, is not destroyed by her involvement in this seamy and dangerous business; she does sink into the lowest depths of poverty and becomes an alcoholic and an opium addict, as well as a prostitute, but she manages to survive and eventually "rise" in the world despite her past. At the conclusion of the novel she is a successful and brilliant actress, highly regarded, wealthy, and philanthropic, but this ending is not intended by Phillips as a "happy ending" in the sentimental sense familiar in so much Hollywood melodrama. Rather, it is a final attack on the middle class values which he exposes throughout the novel, for Susan has succeeded at last by disregarding convention and breaking the rules of a stifling propriety.

The novel has a picaresque form: Susan, born out of wedlock (her mother dies in childbirth) and raised by her uncle and aunt, leaves home after a forced marriage to learn through her subsequent adventures and experiences on the road that at bottom life is sordid and human nature petty and base. Though its heroine is not a rogue or rascal in the classic "picaro" style, Phillips' novel exhibits the realistic flavor and episodic structure of the traditional satiric sub-genre, drawing its main narrative energy from the author's anger and contempt for the corrupt values of his society. Rather like a humorless and finally unrepentant Moll Flanders, Susan witnesses the widespread hypocrisy and injustice of a world dedicated to material gain at the expense of all nobler concepts of virtue and countless human souls.

The novel is very long—perhaps too long—and it abounds in sometimes repetitive incidents, exotic settings, and plentiful characters, its heroine meeting with a rather incredible succession of lurid experiences on the road from unpropitious beginnings to the rewards of fame and fortune. Reared by relatives in a small Indiana river town, Susan is from the first something of a social outcast, marked with the stigma of her "bad blood," for the townspeople are convinced that Susan will turn out like her mother (a "fallen" woman) and that she must suffer for her mother's sins. Extraordinarily beautiful, however, she attracts unintentionally a suitor in whom her jealous cousin is also interested, and when Susan accidentally meets the man in a cemetery while visiting her mother's grave, she is labelled "loose" by her aunt and uncle and forbidden to socialize.

Angered and frustrated by this unfair treatment, Susan runs off to Cincinnati, but her uncle pursues her there and then takes her to another relative's farm to live. Vowing that "we ain't going to have any more bastards in this family," he forces her to marry a local farmer, whom Phillips describes as an animal, in graphic, naturalistic terms:

> He used his knife in preference to his fork, heaping the blade high, packing the food firmly upon it with fork or fingers, then thrusting it into his mouth. He ate voraciously, smacking his lips, breathing hard, now and then eructing with frank energy and satisfaction.[4]

She soon runs away from this boorish husband and on the road meets Roderick Spenser, a Cincinnati journalist. He puts her up in a hotel, but when he fails to return the next day, she joins a showboat—the Floating Palace of Thespians—as a singer. There she is befriended by the manager, Robert Burlingham, and, when the boat is wrecked, they try to break into show business together in Cincinnati. Instead, Burlingham contracts typhoid, and in order to help pay the expenses required to keep him in a private room, Susan prostitutes herself for the first time. Burlingham soon dies, and Susan, for the first time, is really alone.

Susan Lenox: Susan (Greta Garbo) and Rodney (Clark Gable) embrace during a rare moment of happiness.

Thereafter she sinks even lower, living in extreme poverty and working in a paper-box factory. When the tenement house she is living in burns down, she and a girlfriend take to the street, and Susan becomes intoxicated by the world of fine restaurants and high living. After a time her friend goes off to marry one of the men she has met, and Susan looks up Roderick Spenser, who is working for a Cincinnati newspaper, and they resume their relationship. Spenser has ambitions to be a playwright, and, fired by the inspiration he draws from Susan, he resigns his job and takes her with him to New York City. He is unable to produce any work, however, and one of his friends suggests to Susan that she is getting in the way of Roderick's progress. She then decides to leave him, and she is once again alone as Volume I ends.

Susan is able to get a high-paying job as a model but soon quits when she discovers that she also has to sleep with buyers as an inducement for their placing large orders with the firm. She is forced to take to the street again—her personal system of ethics is rather erratic—and is tricked into working for Freddie Palmer, who becomes her "protector" and who is rising in city politics. Now known as Queenie Brown, Susan is soon addicted to alcohol and narcotics. Palmer falls in love with her, but she manages to escape him, only to encounter an even worse fate—drugged in a saloon by a "cadet," she wakes up to find herself in another house of prostitution. She escapes this predicament by frightening the madame with the names of some politicians, and then drifts about aimlessly, sinking deeper into drug addiction. When all hope seems lost, she comes across Roderick Spenser, now a drunk and a derelict, and suddenly she feels that "now she has something to live for," in the hope that rehabilitating him will help her to rehabilitate herself.

Susan is able to nurse Roderick back to health, resorting once more to prostitution to pay his hospital bills. They resume their relationship, and he eventually gets a job in the theater. Through his theater connections, Susan meets

Robert Brent, a famous playwright, who sees great potential in her and makes her his protégée, personally tutoring her for the stage. Susan becomes infatuated with Brent—she especially admires his independence, dedication and genius—and when he unexpectedly takes off for Europe, she feels hurt and deserted (she and Roderick have meanwhile parted company). Now she returns to Freddie Palmer, who has become almost respectable and very wealthy, and they set out to conquer European society. There they meet Brent, who convinces Susan to redirect her energies to the stage. Then Freddie, jealous of Susan's dedication to Brent, has him killed. Susan leaves Freddie, and because Brent has made her his heir, she is free to be independent. The novel concludes with her achievement of fame and success as an actress.

Relying, for the sustainment of interest, on the melodramatics of his plot, Phillips concentrates his critical faculties on exploring societal ills, displaying a rare ability to detail the degradations of poverty and harsh working conditions and to paint realistic scenes of social evil. It is this which distinguishes *Susan Lenox* as a novel and places it above most protest/muckraking literature, which is often very much bound to a certain time and place. Phillips' portraits have an urgency that keeps them relevant beyond their era and a power that evidences the considerable talent and conviction of their creator.

It is her experience in the slums that hardens Susan and teaches her her philosophy of life, the increasingly cynical and deterministic views propounded in the novel. Phillips focuses on the conflict between the weak and the strong, preaches the values of freedom and selfhood over slavery and submission, and examines the important role that accident and chance play in the life of man, demonstrating in frequent narrative asides the profound pessimism of the naturalistic philosopher:

> Those who fancy the human animal is in the custody of some conscious and predetermining destiny think with their vanity

rather than with their intelligence. A careful look at any day or even hour of any life reveals the inevitable influence of sheer accidents, most of them trivial. And these accidents, often the most trivial, most powerfully determine not only the direction but also the degree and kind of force—what characteristics shall develop and what shall dwindle. (p. 240)

Susan, despite her religious upbringing, soon abandons her faith in religion and God, at one point thinking, "No hope, and no reason for hope. No God—and no reason for a God." This dismissal of the concept of God is emphasized often in the novel, Susan's naturalistic credo receiving emphasis in such exchanges as this: a Salvation Army worker having pronounced piously that "the wages of sin is death," Susan replies, "The wages of weakness is death . . . but the wages of sin—well, sometimes it's a house on Fifth Avenue."

Susan is victimized early in life by a rigid, Calvinist view of fate—her mother's sin preordaining that Susan will never be good—and this ultimately serves as the determining force in her flight from the "comfortable" small town of her childhood. Burlingham, the manager of the showboat and one of her earliest reality instructors, provides a naturalist's revision on Calvinist doctrines in his advice to Susan:

You're going to fight your way up to what's called the triumphant class—the people on top—they have all the success, all the money, all the good times. Well, the things you've been taught—at church—in the Sunday school—in the nice storybooks you've read—those things are all for the triumphant class, or for the people working meekly along in 'the station to which God has appointed them' and handing over their earnings to their betters. But those nice moral things you believe in—they don't apply to people like you—fighting their way up from the meek working class to the triumphant class. . . . Once you've climbed up among the successful people you can afford to indulge—in moderation—in practicing the good old moralities. . . . But while you're climbing, no Golden Rule and no turning of the cheek. (pp. 178–79)

Susan begins her picaresque education, like many heroes, on the road, but the road leads nowhere, and finally, like Huck Finn, she boards a boat traveling to river towns. Unlike Huck, however, who finds moments of genuine freedom and enlightenment on the river, Susan's river experiences prove to be no more congenial than her adventures on land. In fact, the boat sinks, and she is forced to enter the world of the modern city, the poorer areas of which are depicted by Phillips as modern hells from which few may escape.

The only possible escape from this world seems to be to doggedly pursue an ethic of freedom and individuality—this lesson is enforced by Robert Brent, another of Susan's "teachers." Brent knows that it is talent alone that may exempt one from the drudgery and wage slavery of the American capitalist system:

> Capitalism divides all men—except those of one class—the class to which I luckily belong—divides all other men into three unlovely classes—slave owners, slave drivers, and slaves. . . . Most human beings . . . have to be in the slave classes. . . . They have to submit to the repulsive drudgery, with no advancement except to slave driver. As for women—if they have to work, what can they do but sell themselves into slavery to the machines, to the capitalists.

To pursue and realize one's talent is to attain the essence of one's individual spirit: "Every one of us has an individuality of some sort. And in spite of everything and anything, except death or hopeless disease, that individuality will insist upon expressing itself."

Unfortunately, the dedicated pursuit of one's talent seems to cut one off from human community, love, and friendship, as one inevitably must concentrate his affections and loyalties on abstractions. Susan recognizes this, and late in the novel reflects on it when thinking about Brent:

> He doesn't care much for people—to have them as intimates. I understand why. Love and friendship bore one—or fail one—

> and are unsatisfactory—and disturbing. But if one centers one's
> life about things—books, pictures, art, a career—why, one is
> never bored or betrayed. He has solved the secret of happiness,
> I think. (p. 635)

Phillips, who was not a persistent intellectual, did not fully
develop this theory, and it remains sketchy; nor does Brent, a
rather sterile character, add any dimension to it. But what
seems to be advocated here, comes very close to Hawthorne's
"unpardonable sin," the breaking away from "the great chain
of humanity." Brent's use of Susan to work out his ideas on
talent and individuality resembles Dr. Rappaccini's relationship with his daughter, a cold, detached, scientific exploitation for the purpose of working out intellectual problems.
Phillips hints that Brent does love Susan but is unable to
express his love—this seeming tension only makes him more
pathetic than "evil," and is one of the novel's more serious
narrative problems. The link with Hawthorne is strengthened
when Susan refers to herself as someone who will "always
wear a veil," suggestive of an alienation from society like that
of Hawthorne's minister. In the financial and emotional
independence and theatrical success that is hers at the end,
Susan achieves success and becomes everything that Brent
could have hoped for, but she has done so by withdrawing
from society. Phillips' concluding words to the novel—"Yes,
she has learned to live. But—she has paid the price."—
remain ambiguous: Susan's "price," ostensibly the suffering
and degradation she suffered before her success, may be
more properly gauged in the permanent communal divorce
that will ensure her independence.

Phillips' philosophy is further muddled by his involving
Susan with an orphanage, which she endows and works for,
thus somewhat mitigating her isolation—though, still, she
touches on human affairs only through an institution, a
convenient abstraction that limits involvement. Furthermore,
the society he depicts in the novel is one that is so hopelessly

corrupt and amoral that one cannot really blame Susan for divorcing herself from it.

Where Phillips' writing and ideas achieve their most perfect union is in his depiction of poverty and its effects on character. The descriptions are moving and powerful, though at times Phillips undercuts his effects by insistently captioning his images with moralizing asides that preach over an achieved dramatic impact. When Susan's tenement house burns down, the homeless, undressed survivors are seen huddled together in a grotesque tableau:

> Even Susan, the most sensitive person there, gazed about with stolid eyes. The nakedness of unsightly bodies, gross with fat or wasted to emaciation, the dirtiness of limbs and torsos long, long unwashed, the foul steam from it all and from the water-soaked rags, the groans of some, the silent, staring misery of others, and, most horrible of all, the laughter of those who yielded like animals to the momentary sense of physical well-being as the heat thawed them out—these sights and sounds together made up a truly infernal picture. And like all the tragedies of abject poverty, it was wholly devoid of that dignity which is necessary to excite the deep pity of respect, was sordid and squalid, moved the sensitive to turn away in loathing rather than to advance with brotherly sympathy and love. (p. 264)

Such frightening spectacles expose in stark relief the substance of raw nature beneath the fragile civilized veneer, violently uncovering the brutish realities of life. Poverty undermines the facade, weakening defenses of refinement, as Susan and her friend Etta discover, for despite their efforts to keep themselves clean and attractive, they are beaten by conditions: "The last traces of civilization were slipping from the two girls; they were sinking to a state of nature." Phillips, who later described the poor as "another race," captures as well the monotonous cycle of their lives and the hopelessness of their situation. Susan experiences it all, and she often contemplates suicide, but her will to live and to rise proves too strong, and if she must compromise herself, it is always to stay alive and pursue her dream.

Intimately connected with the predicament of the poor is the urban industrial system, with its dehumanizing effects on individual and community. Susan suffers through the endless routine of menial, degrading work under barbaric conditions by day, only to return to similar living conditions at night:

> Hundreds, perhaps thousands of girls, at least her equals in sensibility, are caught in the same calamity every year, tens of thousands, ever more and more as our civilization transforms under the pressure of industrialism, are caught in the similar calamities of soul-destroying toil. (p. 442)

Because of her vitality and extraordinary beauty, Susan will not be transformed into a haggard, spiritless skeleton like those around her, but she is an exception, the heroine privileged to break through the cycle of deterioration and defeat, to move on to other scenes and some brighter prospects.

If exposing the living and working conditions of the poor is one of the novel's major themes, its other central concern is the plight of the single woman. Writing at a time when interest in feminist affairs was strong, in his previous novels Phillips had dealt with women's mistreatment and their rights, but in *Susan Lenox* he reveals his sensitive grasp of women's grievances and the problems and hazards they face in the modern world. During this difficult transitional time, when industrialism was taking hold, many families were caught between old-world ideas of the woman as ornament and the need for women to work and succeed in the world like men, and Susan is caught in this dilemma, as she herself recognizes: "I was raised as a lady and not as a human being."

Phillips' primary example of the typical male attitude toward women is Roderick Spenser, one man whom Susan really loves despite his shallowness, selfishness, and promiscuity. There is nothing really attractive about Spenser—he resembles the kind of rake figure popular in eighteenth-century sentimental fiction:

> With his narrowing interest in women—narrowed now almost to sex—his contempt for them as to their minds and their hearts was so far advancing that he hardly took the trouble to veil it with remnants of courtesy. If Susan had clearly understood— even if she had let herself understand what her increasing knowledge might have enabled her to understand—she would have hated him in spite of the hold gratitude and habit had given him upon her loyal nature—and despite the fact that she had, as far as she could see, no alternative to living with him but the tenements or the streets. (p. 328)

The tragedy of woman's experience, as true in Susan's modern world as in the experience of Pamela or Clarissa, is that to maintain some kind of decent standard of living, she must subject herself to this kind of male—if, indeed, she is lucky enough to be attractive and desirable to him—or be forced into a job market which offers her no opportunity but for menial labor and wages insufficient for even the most negligible life style.

The only way to "rise" above the life conditioned by this system was to take to the streets, and many women did so. As in much of the muckraking literature directed against the proliferation of prostitutes and houses of prostitution, Phillips details not only the health hazards of this life, providing descriptions of the ravages of venereal disease, but also the involvement of organized crime in the business—some of these details have as much relevance today as they did at the turn of the century. Operating on her own or with a friend for a short time, Susan finds herself, upon her arrival in New York, quickly taken over by Freddie Palmer, who is only part of a large, complex network of corrupt politicians and police. The women of her street world are threatened with violence, prison terms and death, and menaced still further by the white slave rings. Susan falls victim to all these horrors, in addition to the dependence on alcohol and cocaine which comes along with the work.

Thus the suffering and the degradation caused by a system which exploits the poor and women is clearly portrayed, but while Phillips is a reformer, he offers no real alternative system, nor, despite his attacks on the abuses of capitalism, does he advocate socialism. In fact, he makes few positive suggestions—he does advocate equal rights for women, and equal pay for equal jobs, and radical change in their social status, but these are partial and problematic solutions which fail to get at the major underpinnings of the vicious system itself. His heroine survives because she is attractive and strong-willed enough to fight her way free, and this seems to be Phillips' final reflection on the dilemma: the strong and determined will rise, the rest must suffer until something changes. It is a naturalist's judgment on the sad state of affairs, the ultimate response a matter of resignation, for, having exposed the evil and expressed his anger, Phillips can envision no radical change, no hopeful alternative.

Susan Lenox contains some very powerful passages, but it does not stand up very successfully on the whole. Novelistically, it is not well structured—as Elizabeth Janeway points out, "Susan's adventures . . . take place at the pleasure of the journalist-author and not out of any real fictional development of character or situation."[5] Susan encounters situations that interest Phillips, situations in which he can use her to explore issues and problems relevant to his vision. This causes problems not only with the structure, but with character as well. Susan, as the central character, is the most developed, but even she is hardly a living, breathing character—it is possible to form a very clear picture of what she looks like, but more difficult to assess her values and her private logic. She lacks any real psychological depth, so that when she finally does rise, it hardly seems to matter much. The other characters are even less well developed: Burlingham is merely a mouthpiece for ideas; Spenser is a standard rake, shallow and pathetic; and Brent, whom Susan also loves, remains a shadowy embodiment of Phillips' theories of individualism and personal strength. The novel, finally, is interesting for the sensationalism of its plot rather than for the artistry of its narrative or the realism of its characters.

Phillips is, moreover, guilty of many of the common excesses of the muckrakers, among them an inability to end a scene at its most effective point and let it stand, and a tendency to repeat certain kinds of scenes too often, as if fearful that the audience may not have absorbed his point. His prose verges too often on the preachy and the melodramatic—a glaring example occurs after Susan's rise to fame and a life of luxury, when Phillips has her return once more to the neighborhood of her past only for the purpose of providing the opportunity for one last sermon on the horrors of poverty.

Yet the novel lives in spite of its deficiencies, presenting a striking and realistic portrait of its time, a time not so far removed that its compromises and its trespasses may be forgotten today. Indeed, because many of the failures of the system that concerned Phillips remain yet unsolved, *Susan Lenox* continues to move and to instruct.

The film *Susan Lenox: Her Fall and Rise*, released by MGM in 1931, was formed more by the Depression era and by the needs of its star, Greta Garbo, than by Phillips' novel. Gone are virtually all of Phillips' rollercoaster plot, his thematic concerns—the narrowness of small-town life, the effects of poverty, the exposé of prostitution, the "New Woman"—and most of his characters. In paring down a very lengthy novel to a film that runs barely ninety minutes, the screenwriters eliminated nearly everything, reducing the bounteous cinematic possibilities of Phillips' fiction to a trite and sentimental love story, tempered by some vague sociological implications and some (at least today) silly Freudian symbolism. The film, made at the beginning of the sound era, also suffers from director Robert Z. Leonard's schizophrenic technique: stylistically, it seems very much grounded in silent film method, which conflicts with the palpable reality of the soundtrack. This strange modal dichotomy is evident in the acting as well—Garbo's exaggerated theatrical mannerisms belong to another era, and her heavy-handed delivery betrays her discomfort with the new medium. Her artificial style remains at odds with Clark Gable's relaxed, realistic manner—Gable seems at ease with sound; Garbo clearly is not.

In his study of Depression films, entitled *We're in the Money*, Andrew Bergman points out that one of the characteristics of the films featuring women stars (at least in the beginning of the decade) was that their heroines often had to resort to prostitution to survive.[6] As conditions became more severe and economic opportunities increasingly restricted, both men and women were forced to operate outside the law: men became gangsters; women were driven to prostitution. Bergman cites *Susan Lenox* as an example of the films focused on these fallen women, or "women of the streets"—others are *Blonde Venus* (1932) with Marlene Dietrich, *Safe in Hell* (1931) with Dorothy MacKaill, and *Faithless* (1932) with Tallulah Bankhead—each of them depicts a woman's willingness "to suffer indignities out of an overriding commitment to one man."[7] Bergman goes on to point out that usually the "fall" of the heroine is established early in the film (Garbo moves in with Gable before thirty minutes of the film have elapsed), the Depression setting making the descent credible. Thereafter, he adds, "once any fatal misstep occurred, complete ruin was certain, until a purification was effected which involved a virtual ceding of one's individuality for the love of the male."[8] The choice women have, these films suggested (until Mae West, with her independent image, changed things in 1933), was to find a man to love or fall victim to circumstances and die.

Susan Lenox is faithful to this central pattern: Susan certainly suffers indignities because of her commitment to Rodney Spenser (Gable), as she dedicates her life to finding him and proving herself to him. However, while the film was made and released during the Depression, no deliberate effort is made in it to exploit this possibly significant background—it is actually unclear when the action is taking place. Susan runs away from home and into the arms of Rodney only because of a tyrannical uncle who tries to force her to marry against her will, not because of any economic or psychological effects of the times.

The opening credit sequence features Tchaikovsky's *Romeo and Juliet* in the background, the music underlining the love story theme—though, unlike Shakespeare's ill-fated couple, the film's lovers will come together at last for a Hollywood happy ending. The initial sequences, immediately following, are interestingly composed and visually arresting: snow falling against a night sky is not at all realistic looking, but creates a striking visual effect, much like the close-up shot of whirling snowflakes in a glass paperweight in *Citizen Kane*. Next comes a long-shot of a horse and buggy, a speck in a dark, open, flat landscape, coming towards a house. The visitor, a doctor, is welcomed at the door by a stern-looking Swede named Ohlin (Jean Hersholt). The doctor immediately goes upstairs and into a room outside which sits a woman in black, who looks like a minister of death. Leonard quickly cuts downstairs, and then slowly, at a slightly distorted angle, his camera moves up the stairway again, settling at last on the woman in black.

The doctor emerges from the room, declaring that the mother is dead, but that he thinks he can save the baby. This statement is followed by a close-up of a barrel filled with ice—a hand holding a pot breaks the ice—then a close-up of hands washing, and finally, in silhouette, the doctor trying to revive the baby. Ohlin and his wife, in the foreground, argue about whether the baby, born out of wedlock, should be saved, and the doctor angrily responds that his duty is to save lives, not destroy them. When the baby has been revived, the doctor leaves. There follows a series of shots, also in silhouette, depicting the growth of Helga, that unwelcome child: a young girl is sweeping, then a taller girl is taking off her uncle's boots, and then an even taller girl is carrying logs and emptying them into a bin; finally, a young woman, still in silhouette, is seen washing dishes. When she is summoned by her uncle's voice, this figure at last emerges out of the shadows, providing the first glimpse of Garbo. It is an interesting, visually exciting opening (even today), but, unfortunately, all this dramatic promise bears little relation, stylistically or thematically, to the remainder of the film.

The plot details of the film's beginning adhere to the novel's literal storyline, though not to its spirit. In order to account for Garbo's pronounced accent, the heroine's family have become Swedish, and she herself is known at first as Helga—she acquires the name Susan Lenox only after running away, adopting it as a means to elude her pursuers. Whereas Phillips' Susan is born into a middle-class American family in Indiana, and grows up comfortably there under the care of an uncle and aunt who love her despite the embarrassment of her illegitimacy, the film's sequence of quick shots depicts Helga's upbringing by a malevolent uncle who never wanted her in the first place (as the scene with the doctor makes clear) and who treats her accordingly. The film, moreover, establishes no sense of place like that developed in the novel: the house Helga grows up in seems isolated and quite independent of any specific geographic or social locale. The filmmakers are not interested, as Phillips was, in exploring the mores of small-town life at the turn of the century, or in attributing any of their heroine's difficulties to the prevailing values of the society which includes the film's audience—their purpose is not the critical, controversial aim of Phillips' authorship, but the creation of conventional Hollywood romance.

When Susan/Helga emerges from the shadows, she is

introduced by her uncle to a boorish-looking man named Mondstrum (Alan Hale) whom she is told she must marry. Frightened, she runs upstairs to her room. Since it is raining outside, Ohlin allows Mondstrum to remain inside until it lets up, removing the liquor bottle from the table before retiring to bed. Mondstrum, however, retrieves the liquor, and after fortifying himself with a few drinks, lurches upstairs in search of Helga—again, this sequence is handled in a visually exciting way, more in keeping with a suspense film than a love story (Leonard's dramatic use of stairways rather resembles the fear-inducing technique that Hitchcock would develop later). Then, Leonard effectively exploits light and shadow contrasts as he cuts from a menacing Mondstrum in the doorway to Helga crouched in a corner of her room. She is able to get away because of his drunkenness, and runs from the house into the storm.

This incident is borrowed from the book, but, like the conditions of the heroine's childhood, substantially changed. All the contributing circumstances with which Phillips establishes the credibility of Susan's plight—her cousin's jealousy, the unfair accusation of "loose" behavior, her escape to Cincinnati and subsequent removal to another family, her forced marriage to the farmer—all this realistic detail is flattened in the film narrative to Helga's nightmarish persecution by the two ogres, Ohlin and Mondstrum. The blatantly melodramatic quality of her flight from the grotesque Mondstrum (monster) forms an appropriate climax to this first part of the film, in which most of the action has developed according to the primarily visual (there has been very little dialogue) silent film techniques of bold editing, radical camera angles, and stagy lighting.

From this point on, the film moves off in a new direction, suddenly shifting to the more realistic style of sound film, and, at the same time, all but abandoning the novel from which it takes its name. Helga runs off in the storm until she comes to the house of Rodney Spenser. The filmmakers slightly alter the name of this character; here even the remotest similarity ends. In the film this man becomes the heroine's true and lasting love, as all of the other lovers of Phillips' Susan are either made cardboard villains or omitted entirely (most notably Robert Brent, whose philosophical teachings and artistic sponsorship could have no place in this streamlined, simplistic love story). In keeping with his new prominence, and with Gable's co-star billing, Rodney's character has undergone a thorough revision, emerging here as a charming and sincere bachelor-about-the-countryside, enough an idealist to be drastically and permanently embittered later by Helga's apparent betrayal. According to Lyn Tornabene in a recent biography of Gable, the filmmakers' intention here was to tone down their co-star's natural "rough, tough image," and "to turn Gable into a Robert Montgomery-Leslie Howard figure of chaste sophistication, yet retain enough of Gable to satisfy his fans."[9] The metamorphosis was not entirely successful, for it merely dilutes the impact of Phillips' rake figure without providing a convincing role for Gable or even an effective foil for Garbo's stylized appeal.

Rodney takes in the shy and inarticulate Helga, insists that she stay and get out of her wet clothes, and offers her a pair of pajamas. They sit at a table by the fire and talk, Rodney revealing that he is an engineer (not a newspaperman, as in the novel) and that he is working on sketches to be entered in a competition. This dialogue sequence is shot in classic Hollywood style, cutting from one speaker to the other, mostly in medium shots, varying this with occasional shots that include both; Garbo's face is usually bathed in light, Gable is photographed more naturally, in keeping with his acting style. He is associated, in a number of shots, with his dog, whose pointed ears resemble Gable's in a curious way—the naturalistic reference is striking, in direct contrast to the sentimental glamor of Garbo's presentation.

The next morning, which is ushered in by some leftover

signs from the silent days—a window shade going up to let in light, then a cut to a coffee pot on a stove—Rodney finds Helga cooking him breakfast and asks her to stay. She agrees, and they spend the afternoon fishing. The fishing sequence is, again, well photographed but weighted down by some heavy-handed Freudian symbolism: she holds a fishing rod and he tells her, "Don't shake it around, you'll never catch anything that way." The symbolism becomes even more embarrassing when Helga, having trouble reeling in the fish, lets it fall on land and then tries to catch it with her hands, giggling as it wriggles out of her hand. Rodney then embraces her and they kiss. The camera, catching Garbo's beautiful face in close-up, ignores Gable—this is one of a number of sequences in which he seems to be treated as an intruder in Garbo's movie.

The scene then shifts to Rodney packing his bag, ready to set off to present his sketches in the engineering competition. He promises Helga, who is now living with him, that he will be back in a few days. Reluctant to part with him, Helga lingers over a picture of Rodney's parents and says that she realizes now that her mother was a good woman even though she didn't have a ring. Rodney promises to bring her a ring and assures her that his parents will love her. This moment of Hollywood sentimentality seems to be an attempt to legitimize their love affair—already portrayed as a healthy, happy, outdoorsy kind of relationship—unofficially betrothing the lovers in the context of families and pledges of faith (neither his parents nor her mother will be of any further concern to them, though the ring will later serve as a convenient token of their lost innocence).

She rides part of the way with Rodney, and then returns to find her uncle and Mondstrum waiting for her at the house. Ohlin tries to force her to go back, but when Rodney's dog attacks him, Helga manages to escape in her uncle's horse and buggy. The shot of her driving away looks like a chariot scene out of *Ben Hur*, ridiculously out of place in this film. She rides to a town called Lenoxville, where she accidently boards a circus train and is given the name Susan Lenox by the tattooed lady. Here she meets Burlingham (John Miljan), the manager, who gives her a job and then—after hiding her in his room from her pursuers—rapes her. The circus troop is, of course, simply a picturesque variation on the acting troupe Susan joins in the novel, but Burlingham has been transformed from the kind man who was her first good friend, into a stock, mustache-twisting villain. The film heroine's real "fall" begins here.

When next seen, Susan is part of the circus sideshow, dancing as "El Fatima" in a black veil. During the break in one show she goes backstage and finds Rodney in her dressing room. They embrace and Susan prepares to leave with him, but, unfortunately, Burlingham walks in at the wrong moment and his words to Susan make Rodney suspicious. Accusing her of being unfaithful, he throws the wedding ring he has brought with him on the ground and tells her to stay in the gutter. Susan then hardens, suddenly claiming that she "always hated men, and from now on it will be different," that if she is to stay in the gutter, she will make it worthwhile. In this scene the disparity in acting styles is especially grating— Garbo's theatrical mannerisms and histrionic tone seem frankly ridiculous in such bold contrast with Gable's clipped, brash style.

Next, Leonard contrives more Freudian sexual imagery, projecting a series of circle images in quick succession to indicate passage of time and Susan's convoluted fall. A close-up of train wheels, over which is superimposed a shot of Susan being picked up in a train, is followed by a circular design on a dance floor, with dancers performing a Busby Berkeley-like number around it and in it. Susan's face is superimposed on this as well, before giving way to a roulette wheel and then a clock ticking off the minutes to the New Year. During this last sequence, Susan is shown descending a stairway with Tom Kelly, the political boss.

Leonard next cuts to Rodney, who is working on an engineering site—he looks disgusted and dissipated, and he is being bawled out by his boss for the faulty design of a bridge which has collapsed—he is fired for his drunken incompetence. During this sequence there is a close-up of a revolving cement mixer whose spout is spewing out cement—an obvious masturbation image. This is immediately followed by a cut to another circle image, this time an elevator floor indicator, then another, a view of the floor, decorated with circular tiles, of a penthouse apartment. Here Kelly and Susan, now his mistress, are giving a party. (Kelly bears a peripheral resemblance to the novel's Freddie Palmer, who also rises to become a political boss, but he is a much younger man than Kelly, and Susan lives with him in Europe, not the U.S.)

It becomes clear that Susan has been following Rodney's failures and has had him mysteriously invited to the party. Rodney, however, becomes offended by Kelly and angered by Susan's disgrace, and he stalks out. Susan quickly decides to leave Kelly, tries to find Rodney but can't, and begins a lengthy search for him. Once again train wheels whirl in the background as a series of names of American cities appears on the screen to indicate Susan's travels, ending, finally, in "Puerto Sacate." Significantly, as Susan continues to fall, she moves further and further south, until she reaches a *hot* tropical climate. Here she is employed in a disreputable brothel-like resort, where she waits for Rodney to return from an upriver work camp. When at last he appears, a drunken and dishevelled laborer, she confronts him again and tells him of her dedication, assuring him that "since I last saw you, no man has had me." He is not yet ready to forgive, however, and walks away, leaving her to blandishments of an unlikely, smitten yachtsman, who offers to take her away from all this. She is tempted, but true love must triumph, so she goes to confront Rodney once more. The final scene shows a much more presentable Rodney packing his bag, the shot focusing on the open bag echoing that earlier in the film when he was packing to leave Susan for the first time. Susan enters—they are both dressed in white—and begs him to stay with her: "We are two cripples clinging to each other—only together can we remain straight." Rodney again expresses doubt about their future, but when Susan declares dramatically, "I'll make you believe in me," they embrace, as the film ends.

Thus Phillips' sprawling and ambitious novel is turned into a clumsily romanticized tale of lovers separated by misunderstanding, suffering hardship and adversity until, through the dedication of the woman, they are once again united. The film is a failure on a number of levels. No merely unintelligent adaptation, the final product seems to indicate that no real attempt was made to preserve, or even to exploit, Phillips' work. The film script was apparently the subject of a great deal of disagreement—no fewer than fourteen writers worked on it[10]—which may explain not only the conflicting energies of the film, but its lack of coherent structure and the weak motivation of its leading characters. Stylistically, it is eccentric and inconsistent, opening with a visually interesting introductory sequence, which, unfortunately, is quite irrelevant to the subsequently developed theme and story. The film seems to be caught in a limbo world of changing styles and techniques, a victim of the transition from silents to sound movies.

The failure of *Susan Lenox* is a glaring one in light of its issuance from MGM, the richest, most productive, and probably the greatest studio of the decade. Considering the wealth of talent at their disposal, and the fact that Phillips' novel had all the ingredients for cinematic success, it is a frustrating misadventure. The film, and surely Garbo, might have been more successful under Clarence Brown, who did such a fine job with *Anna Christie* in 1930 and would later guide her through *Anna Karenina* in 1935.[11] His ability to capture the spirit of America through landscape and personality in a film like *Human Hearts* (1938) shows what he might have been able to do with Phillips' rural and urban land-scapes. Robert Z. Leonard, on the other hand, was a studio worker who never did very distinguished work. He is remembered primarily for his uncharacteristically strong 1940 adaptation of Jane Austen's *Pride and Prejudice* (whose success, in fact, lies more in Aldous Huxley and Jane Murfin's very literate script and in the excellent matching of its two stars, Greer Garson and Laurence Olivier, than in his direction).

MGM, however, was more a star's studio than a director's studio, and the film does not display the firm hand of a director in control—it is a star's vehicle. Garbo insisted on Clark Gable, and this, in part, was the unmaking of the film, as their acting styles remain incompatible. In conjunction with the radical retailoring of Phillips' novel to fit the star, this undisciplined and uncoordinated approach could not succeed.

3

SPECIAL DELIVERY

THE NOVEL
The Postman Always Rings Twice
(1934, James M. Cain)

THE FILM
The Postman Always Rings Twice
(1946, Tay Garnett)

James M. Cain did not see the film version of his novel *The Postman Always Rings Twice* until 1976—thirty years after it was released; his reaction then was, "I was surprised that it was no worse than it was."[1] Cain, to be sure, was no fan of the movies, his basic attitude summed up by a character in another of his novels, *Serenade:* "Understand for my money, no picture is any good, really any good." In an interview shortly before his death he recalled the genesis of this disaffection: "When we were boys, a friend and I walked downtown to this nickelodeon. . . . The feature was *The Great Train Robbery*. I had no idea that this was moving picture history. To us it was utterly beyond belief, it was so lousy. We came out agreeing it was not good entertainment, but it passed the time. Movies pretty much affect me this way now."[2]

Although Cain himself was not a successful screenwriter, his novels and stories have provided the basis for some of Hollywood's most popular films. *Double Indemnity* (1943) is perhaps the best film made from his work, and it started the trend of "high-budget private-eye pictures."[3] *Mildred Pierce* (1945) won Joan Crawford an Academy Award. *Root of his Evil* (1951) was made twice, once as *When Tomorrow Comes* (1938) and later as *Interlude* (1956). His best novel, *The Postman Always Rings Twice*, has inspired three different films: a French version, *Le Dernier Tournant* (1939), Luchino Visconti's unauthorized Italian version, *Ossessione* (1942), and the American version, released in 1946, which retained Cain's original title.

The Postman Always Rings Twice (1934) was Cain's first published novel, and it remains as his best, successfully combining the basic elements of theme and story which made and have kept him famous. In his preface to *The Butterfly* (1947) he explains that his novels revolve thematically around "the wish that comes true"; this, he says, is a "terrifying concept, at least to my imagination. Of course the wish must really have terror in it." He claims Pandora, "the first woman," as his inspiration:

> I think my stories have some quality of the opening of a forbidden box, and it is this, rather than violence, sex, or any of the things usually cited by way of explanation, that gives them the drive so often noted. Their appeal is first to the mind, and the reader is carried along as much by his own realization that the characters cannot have this particular wish and survive, and his curiosity to see what happens to them, as by the effect on him of incident, dialogue, or character. Thus, if I do any glancing, it is towards Pandora, the first woman, a conceit that pleases me, somehow, and often helps my thinking.[4]

Another apt metaphor for the typical situation in a Cain

novel comes from Edmund Wilson's discussion of Cain in "The Boys in the Back Room":

> Cain's heroes are capable of extraordinary exploits, but they are always treading the edge of a precipice; and they are doomed, like the heroes of Hemingway, for they will eventually fall off the precipice. But . . . the hero of a novel by Cain is an individual of mixed unstable character, who carries his precipice with him like Pascal.[5]

The image of the precipice suggests the aura of doom which permeates Cain's best work, as his characters set in motion a series of events which must end in destruction. The horror of the situation is in the wish itself, for it is always in reality a death-wish, a barely concealed desire to plunge from the precipice—Huff, the protagonist of *Double Indemnity* even describes the woman who fascinates him as looking like "what came aboard the ship to shoot dice for the souls in 'The Rime of the Ancient Mariner.'" Unlike Hemingway, to whom he is often compared, Cain indulges in no sense of tragedy, however, but remains steadily objective about his characters, as if leaving them alone to be their stupid, common selves and to suffer the consequences of situations created by their own natures.

This sounds rather existential, and of course it is; Cain, like McCoy, was "discovered" first in France, acclaimed especially by the Existentialists. Camus' *L'Etranger,* writes Richard Lehan, "owes a significant literary debt to a work like James Cain's *The Postman Always Rings Twice,*"[6] and W. M. Frohock claims that Camus paid Cain "the compliment of imitation."[7] In America, however, Cain is regularly denounced by critics as a writer of pulp fiction that caters to an unsophisticated audience. Frohock's remark that "nothing he wrote was completely outside the category of trash,"[8] and Albert Van Nostrand's contention that Cain's characters lack thought or feeling[9] are typical.

Some distinguished readers do rise to defend Cain, even in America. Edmund Wilson conceded him to be the best of the "poets of the tabloid murder" and found in him "enough of the real poet" to redeem his work as literature.[10] David Madden has written many perceptive pieces on Cain, including a booklength study in which he correctly argues that critics should evaluate Cain according to what he sets out to do, not what they think he ought to have attempted.[11] Other admirers include Tom Wolfe, Stephen King ("Everyone should study him in writing class, instead of the marsh gas they put out for us to admire."), Ross Macdonald and John Macdonald. Most recently, Roy Hoops, in an appreciation of Cain in *The New Republic*, calls him a "writer's writer."[12]

The quintessential Cain novel, *Postman*, is certainly rich enough to be enjoyed on several levels. As a thirties novel, somewhat colored by the Depression (though not proletarian in any political sense), it can be read as an exploration of the American dream, which is exposed as an empty sham. The novel's protagonist, Frank Chambers, is a not very intelligent member of the proletariat trying to deal with Depression America. Madden calls him "a simple-minded Whitman," for he is in love with the open road and a life of movement; he is out of place in modern, technological America. Frank, though, is not really pursuing any dream of freedom on the road, but just moving along, aimlessly drifting from town to town. The novel's opening line, typical of Cain's terse, suggestive style, at once characterizes Frank and hints at the violence that is to come: "They threw me off the truck about noon." His life of carefree freedom (a very male and very American dream) is to be challenged almost immediately when he meets Cora, the wife of the owner of a roadside diner. Fatally attracted, he will try to get her to share his life and his dream:

"Just you and me and the road, Cora."
"Just you and me and the road."

"Just a couple of tramps."
"Just a couple of gypsies, but we'll be together."
"That's it. We'll be together."[13]

Cora, however, seeks another side of the American dream—the dream of success, of being "somebody." Having won a beauty contest in Iowa, she has come to Los Angeles in the hope of becoming a movie star. Like many others, she found not stardom but a betrayal of her dream—in this, as in his other California novels, Cain shows how the hopes of the western movement collapsed beneath the California sunshine and shattered on the shores of the Pacific. Now married to a man she detests, Cora is a cook and waitress in his cheap, tawdry diner.

During moments of passion she invariably agrees to go along with Frank's schemes to "light out for the territory" and live the carefree, irresponsible life of the wanderer. But in the light of day, reality intervenes, and she realizes that life on the road is not for her. One time she actually does go with Frank, but after a couple of miles decides to turn back, explaining, "I told you I wasn't really a bum, Frank. I don't feel like no gypsy. I don't feel like nothing, only ashamed, that I'm out here asking for a ride" (p. 25). Still possessed of her essentially middle-class ambitions, Cora dreams of turning the diner into a thriving, respectable business: "I want to work and be something, that's all. But you can't do it without love." She will try to do it with murder instead.

Cora and Frank make two attempts to murder her husband, the Greek, and the second time they succeed. The trial that follows is a comment on the American concept of justice, as the prosecutor and the defense attorney play cat-and-mouse, crossing and double-crossing each other in trying to win the case. The sense of corruption is pervasive, so that when they are at last acquitted, Frank remarks that Cora looks "like the great grandmother of every whore in the world" (p. 76). Thus Cain explores through his ill-met lovers

The Postman Always Rings Twice: Cora (Lana Turner) confronts Frank
(John Garfield), igniting a passion that will lead to their destruction.

the violent potential of the American experience, as the dream of freedom and the dream of upward mobility collide head on, breeding death and destruction.

The more fruitful approach to the novel, however, lies in its development of basic existential themes. Frohock, for instance, writes that "a Cain character, like a good existentialist, was what he did."[14] The characters are largely developed through their actions—Frank is always in motion, always doing something—and Cain avoids any discursive pauses that might interfere with the movement of his story. Not the least of the novel's accomplishments is in the sheer force of this headlong narrative, its very momentum moving the reader along, almost against his will, from one episode to the next, compelling, in Madden's words, an "almost complete emotional commitment to the traumatic experiences Cain renders."[15]

Madden accurately labels Cain's works examples of the "pure novel," for narrative action, not philosophy, is the major element of his storytelling. All his creative energy is directed toward getting the story told "as briefly and forcibly as possible. . . . The novel should raise and answer its own necessary questions and depend as little as possible upon anything beyond the bounds of its own immediacy."[16] In *Serenade* Cain suggests an analogy to musical technique that sums up his own novelistic values:

Beethoven, Mendelssohn, Puccini, Mascagni, Bizet, and such men are my favorites, all different emotionally, but similar in the logic of their musical approach. Wagner, Richard Strauss, Debussy, and such men, who depend on an overpowering gush of tone, harmony, and color, tend to bore me. It even carries over to the popular side, for Vincent Youmans interests me more than any American composer. "Tea for Two" is a thematic building of tune out of three notes treated as a theme. It, therefore, to my imagination, is exciting, all the more so because of its leanness, and the avoidance of any surplus, even to one grace note.

More than any of his other novels, *Postman* is a realization of this implied credo: within the first six pages Frank arrives at the diner, gets a job, meets Cora, and makes love to her; five pages later they have decided to kill the Greek and have put the plan into action. There is no surplus, not even a "grace note" to fill out the scene, and yet Cain is able to pursue his theme with a conviction of realism that grows from the narrow-focused "immediacy" of his vision.

Frank, who narrates the novel, embodies the sense of fatal urgency that animates Cain's world. He has no past but functions entirely within the present, and his narration proceeds without reflection. As Richard Lehan points out, Frank "reacts rather than acts": he sees Cora, he wants her, and he goes after her; because her husband stands in the way of gratification of his sexual desire, he plans to kill him. Unchecked by any moral compunction, he behaves consistently in the manner of an animal—eating, drinking, and fornicating seem to define the limits of his universe. One of his first actions in the novel is to order breakfast, and Cain, who spares no time for irrelevant detail, has him itemize the meal of a foraging beast: "He layed a place at one of the tables and asked me what I was going to have. I said orange juice, corn flakes, fried eggs and bacon, enchilada, flapjacks, and coffee" (p. 3). When he meets Cora, he displays an equally voracious sexual appetite, which is linked ironically with his desire for food: "I wanted that woman so bad I couldn't even keep anything on my stomach" (p. 71). The description of their first embrace, too, underscores the feral energy of his response to these appetites: "I took her in my arms and mashed my mouth up against hers . . . 'Bite me! Bite me!' I bit her. I sunk my teeth into her lips so deep I could feel the blood spurt into my mouth. It was running down her neck when I carried her upstairs" (p. 9). The animalism of his behavior in such scenes clearly establishes the potential violence of this man's reaction to the pressure of his physical desires.

An air of doom pervades the novel, accentuated by the recurrent influence of chance, accident and coincidence in the plot development. At its end he has been sentenced to death for murdering Cora, although her death, in an automobile crash, was in fact entirely accidental. Frank narrates his story from his prison cell, and at its conclusion he insists on accepting responsibility for his actions:

> There's a guy in no. 7 that murdered his brother, and says he really didn't do it, his subconscious did it. . . . God almighty, I can't believe that! . . . To hell with the subconscious. I don't believe it. It's just alot of hooey, that this guy thought up just to fool the judge. You know what you're doing, and you do it. (p. 101)

His thoughts still focused on Cora, Frank recognizes that his own lust and desire precipitated the events that have ensnared him and that he is, in fact, guilty even though Cora's death was accidental. No concern for forgiveness by man or God bothers him—he is even suspicious of the priest who attends him (earlier he found his own natural religion in sex: "I kissed her. Her eyes were shining up at me like two blue stars. It was like being in church" [p. 14]). To Cora herself he has already acknowledged his sense of the absurdity of human existence: "We thought we were on top of a mountain. That wasn't it. It's on top of us and that's where it's been ever since that night" (p. 94). Doomed by his own nature, he has played out his destructive role in a meaningless drama, and at its end he is left alone to confront a fate for which he is responsible, without having ever had any power to change it.

Unlike many existential works, *Postman* is not a novel of ideas. No concrete philosophical point of view is developed or discussed; Madden even suggests that Cain's absurdist vision might have been an unconscious one: "Whether Cain is aware of it or not, the persistence of his theme is real enough in his work to show that he feels the truth of the concept but does not feel compelled to preach it."[17] However, as Cain himself recognized in proposing the conceit of Pandora's box, the essence of his thematic drive and of his narrative art lies in the dramatic energy of fatality, underlying the concept of the disguised death wish that animates his characters. In pursuit of forbidden desires they enmesh themselves in a train of events whose end comes with terrifying swiftness and violence. In Cain's *Postman* Frank and Cora move inexorably from a self-centered hell to violent death.

In his family tree of *film noir*, Raymond Durgnat classifies *Postman* under "middle-class murder" and further describes it as a film dealing with "the corruption of the not-so-innocent male," its action modeled on the Clytemnestra plot of classical myth.[18] Tay Garnett's version of the Cain novel is lacking, however, in certain essentials of this genre, whose characteristic evocation of terror depends upon a consistency of vision and effect that compels recognition, finally, of a pervasive evil infecting the world in which the characters move. *Postman* does not share the perpetually dark, rainy, foggy, or wet atmosphere which embodies and intensifies the fearful tension of such films' drama. On the contrary, most of its action takes place in bright sunlight, which tends, unfortunately, to dissipate the impression of fatal passion on which Cain's story depends.

Only once, in what is the film's most effective scene, does Garnett's camera manage to present a graphic image of the impending doom that shadows his characters. On a dark, foggy night, Cora and Frank drive along a coast highway, readying themselves to kill her husband, Nick. The scene opens on a long shot, discovering the car, which appears as a mere speck, precariously balanced on the narrow road; one side of the highway abuts a steep cliff, the other an endless drop. The dramatic composition of this shot provides a brief, startling glimpse of the world of the *film noir*, embodying in ominous darkness the frightened, doubtful, and pessimistic mood of the forties. It remains an isolated effect, as the scene soon reverts to the incongruous daytime setting in which the violent drama is to be played out.

The film does, however, attempt to exploit a significant subsidiary feature of the *film noir* genre, the dominant woman whose driving ambition threatens the male world. Such "bitch goddesses"—elsewhere termed "monsters and harpies"—were typically, according to Stephen Farber,

> . . . hardened by greed and lust, completely without feeling for the suffering they caused. These films undoubtedly reflected the fantasies and fears of a wartime society, in which women had taken control of many of the positions customarily held by men. Fear of the violence that may attend success is a recurring anxiety in American films, but during the war years another psychological dimension was added to this anxiety—fear of the evil, overpowering woman with a shocking ability to humiliate and emasculate her men.[19]

Postman's Cora, as portrayed by Lana Turner, is not as ruthless as this, although it is her determination to better herself and to use Frank to do so that sets them both on the course to death and disaster. Either because, in expanding the role to suit her star status, the filmmakers reconceived Cain's amoral temptress, or because Turner was not actress enough to project an intensity of evil, her Cora possesses a vulnerability that counteracts the drive of her ambition and so sacrifices the clarity of the conventional villainess role. Most likely, as Richard Dyer suggests, Turner's public could not have accepted her in a thoroughly negative role because of the strong sympathy engendered by her troubled personal life:

> The particular inflection she adds is suffering from one's own impulses. Her impulsive marriages in life had led to suffering of one kind and another, and the film roles reprised this.

Consequently the pattern of impulse and entrapment in *Post-man* can be read—I would argue, *was* read by Turner's fans—as a source of identification and sympathy. The attraction to bad (often meaning little more than sexual desire) can be seen as an uncontrollable destroying impulse that anyone can identify with (especially in a sex-negative culture).[20]

This expanded conception of the woman's part creates a major problem in the film version—it is never clear who (or, finally, what) the story is about. Frank (John Garfield) is occasionally heard as narrator, and, like the novel, the film does end with him in jail talking to a priest; because it retains this basic structure, this *Postman,* too, would seem to focus on the hero's doom. However, Cora has now been made as impor-tant a character as Frank, and she initiates at least as much of the action as he does. The centrality of her desires is hinted at in the beginning, when the camera focuses on the "Man Wanted" sign that draws Frank to the diner: he almost seems to show up at her request. Soon afterwards, Frank is seen burning the sign, as if to show that he *is* Cora's man. Then, later, she is the one who decides to murder Nick, and when the first attempt fails, she is given a motivation (not in the novel) to try a second time. This purposefulness, coupled with her desire to improve herself and expand the business, makes her a commanding and dynamic figure.

Frank, on the other hand, here becomes weak and indecisive, robbed of that animal-sexual drive which made him a compelling force in the novel's action. The difference is neatly demonstrated in the episode of the second murder attempt. In the novel, after Frank has killed Nick, they push the car over the cliff; then he turns on Cora, rips open her blouse, and has sex with her, before sending her up the hill to find help; finally, he manipulates the car to make it fall on him, hoping to prove to the police that all this has been accidental and that Frank was lucky to escape alive. In the film, Frank kills Nick, but when he attempts to push the car over the cliff, he falls over with it, almost killing himself. Bumbling into an appearance of innocence, whereas Cain's protagonist deliberately created it, the film's Frank seems merely awkward rather than doomed.

Frank's masculine bravado is further undercut in the scene in which he is bullied into a confession by the district attorney, Sackett. In the novel, Frank does finally surrender to Sackett's insistent questioning, but only after an extended resistance. The D.A.'s victory comes much more easily in the film, and the camera's focus on Frank's frightened face further emphasizes his weakness. This undermining of Frank's compulsive personality makes little sense in terms of the story, for it only confuses the impression of self-destructive energy that animates the novel. Consequently, Garfield, who was certainly capable of portraying the brutal, obsessive Frank Chambers of Cain's conception, instead seems as confused as the character he is portraying.

Thus deprived of Frank's fatal drive, and further burdened with an ambivalent Cora, the film version is static, dull, and unexciting. Although its running time is less than two hours, it seems overly long, its narrative unfocused and equivocal. The film's opening is indicative of this problem: whereas Cain's first sentence is taut, suggestive of violence, revelatory of Frank's character and the accidental nature of his world, the film begins blandly, as a decently dressed, unhurried Frank is dropped off in front of the diner by Sackett. He even seems to be in search of work, and so, when he quickly decides to stay, it is not immediately clear whether it is the allure of Cora (emphatically Frank's object in the novel) or simply the prospect of a job that has influenced this fateful choice.

Cora's first appearance in the film is justly famous: a tube of lipstick rolls along the floor, attracting both Frank's and the camera's attention; the slow track back along the floor, up her bare legs, shorts, and halter top, is frankly sensual, its visual impact heightened in the contrast of her crisp, white clothes against a shadowy background. The hard whiteness suggests the heat of the sun and reinforces the bright lighting of the film; like Melville's "whiteness of the whale," Cora's white-hot radiance seems to symbolize the mysterious, frightening, and irresistible nature of her evil influence as her sexuality is manifested to Frank, and to the viewer, in an almost blinding visual image.

This well-conceived, tantalizing introduction is promising, but its creative flare soon fades into ponderous exposition as the filmmakers proceed to translate Cain's explosive, sex-driven tale into the heavy-handed, melodramatic conventions common to forties film. The lovers' animal sexuality, of course, had to be toned down, but this Frank is hardly even seen to kiss Cora; not even the scenes on the beach (again beautifully lit) have any real suggestive quality. Instead, when Frank first sees Cora, there is a clumsy montage sequence of a burning hamburger on the grill, apparently meant to suggest sizzling passion. Having thus deadened the physical impetus which inspired the novel's action, the film version must rely instead on an elaborate set of rational motivations for its characters' behavior, although the provision of such reasons considerably weakens the thematic structure and slows down the pace.

For example, Cora's desire to be rid of her husband receives much more deliberate justification in the film than is supplied in the novel. When Cain's Frank explains simply that being married to a Greek has made Cora feel "she wasn't white," he locates the murder in his own crude and callous world. Nick, in fact, seems to be a rather amiable fellow; Frank is even moved to weep at his funeral: "I got to blubbering while they were letting him down. Singing those hymns will do it to you every time, and specially when it's about a guy you liked as well as I liked the Greek" (p. 73). The murder, clearly, has been prompted solely by the overriding lust and ambition of two individuals who are horribly indifferent to their victim's humanity. The purity of Cain's focus is lost in the transition to film, however, as the screenwriters struggle awkwardly to mitigate Cora's crime.

Her motive is modified—she now feels trapped in marriage to the older man (he is no longer a Greek, but renamed Smith), whom she married in the first place because she was tired of being bothered by other men—and this sense of entrapment is further reinforced by the portrayal of Nick as a cheap, penny-pinching, stupid, and unlikeable man. After the first attempt to kill him fails, Cora is provided with yet another incentive for murder when Nick declares his intention to sell the diner—her ambition to better herself has centered on the improvement and expansion of the diner—and to take her back to Canada to care for his invalid sister. (At this point, even the audience is looking forward to this ogre's death.)

Not only does all of this superfluous, and heavily clichéd, rationalizing detract from the impression of the headlong race toward doom which is Cain's thematic focus, but it also undermines the film's own coherence. In trying too hard to make Cora sympathetic by making Nick so thoroughly repulsive, the filmmakers collide with their simultaneous attempt to exploit the "bitch goddess" type of *film noir*: the same woman whose situation has been rendered so clearly intolerable is yet made unattractive in her coarse ambitiousness, her calculating sexuality, her perverse delight in confessing to the murder in order to implicate Frank as well. Rather than combining finally to suggest the mysterious, "unknowable" quality of the dominant female's evil, these contradictory impulses of characterization serve only to obscure the meaning of her actions and thus of the story itself.

The tedious development of conventional motivation also undercuts the filmmakers' attempts to salvage something of Cain's metaphysical statement. During the scenes in which Cora and Frank contemplate murder, their direst thoughts are invariably accompanied by a crashing musical score, presumably to indicate the irrational violence of their passion. The original inspiration for the crime is provided in a scene invented for the film: a drunken Nick almost smashes his car into a truck; Frank remarks, "I'd like to see him get plastered like that and drive off a cliff"; the music swells dramatically as Cora answers tensely, "You didn't mean that—you were joking." Dyer identifies the recurrent pattern of such episodes: "The idea for murder arises spontaneously, music signals its impact, a kiss links it to passion."[21] The ineptness of this overworked sequence—the lovers are required to reenact the scene of inspiration twice, in detail—is not helped by the underplaying of their sexual dynamism. Despite Dyer's assertion, there is nothing spontaneous about these elaborately motivated thoughts of murder, and so little passion has been displayed in the relationship of the plotters that it is difficult to believe that they have been suddenly overcome by any such irrational force. The orchestral fanfare signals only a mechanical turn in a plot overloaded with contradictory impulses.

Another awkward effort to preserve Cain's atmosphere of doom involves the use of Sackett (Leon Ames), the district attorney who interrogates and then prosecutes Frank in the novel. In the film version Sackett becomes curiously omnipresent: he drops off Frank at the diner at the story's opening; he appears at the hospital after the failed first murder attempt; he picks up Cora on the coast road after the second, successful one; he is with Frank in the jail cell at the end. As a device contrived to suggest the murderers' inescapable fate, this character's unlikely ubiquity becomes monotonous and finally even unintentionally comic; it intrudes on the narrative rather than giving it any thematic strength.

The ending of the film adds to the confusion by trying to provide the audience a Hollywood happy ending. As in the novel, Cora learns that she is pregnant and decides to forgive Frank for an episode of infidelity. Deciding to test his love, she takes him to the beach and gets him to swim out with her so far into the sea that she is too exhausted to return without his help. She tells him that he can simply let her drown and be done with her, but he rescues her and thus proves his love. In the novel, Frank explains,

> I looked at the green water. And with my ears ringing and that weight on my back and chest, it seemed to me that all the devilment, and meanness, and shiftlessness, and no-account stuff in my life had been pressed out and washed off, and I was all ready to start out with her again clean, and do like she said, have a new life. (p. 97)

This purification scene is also handled well in the film. The scene is shot in dark shadow: Frank and Cora run into the ocean; there is a medium shot of their heads bobbing in the water as she offers him the chance to abandon her, then a long shot of Frank carrying Cora back to the car. They reaffirm their love while driving back home, but, in an amorous moment Frank takes his eyes off the road and crashes the car into a fence. The last shot of Cora shows one arm dangling from the seat, the limp hand releasing her lipstick, which rolls onto the car's floor. The reappearance of the lipstick tube thus neatly recalls her torrid introductory sequence; the skillful visual symbolism of these frame scenes unfortunately points up the weakness of the staging of most of the intermediate action.

Frank is, ironically, convicted of murdering Cora. In the novel, he faces his death stoically and attempts to sort and figure things out, though he is not very good at it. (Joyce Carol Oates remarks that the "Cain hero is no more metaphysically inclined than he is morally substantial."[22]) He fantasizes about meeting Cora in some afterlife, so that he can reassure her of his love:

> But that's the awful part, when you monkey with murder. Maybe it went through her head, when the car hit, that I did it anyhow. That's why I hope I've got another life after this one. Father McConnell says I have, and I want to see her. I want her to know that it was all so, what we said to each other, and that I didn't do it. (p. 100)

Cain's Frank enjoys dreaming about such an afterlife, but he really doesn't believe the priest, and "when I start to figure, it all goes blooey." When he ends his confession and asks the reader to pray for him, the novel ends with the suggestion that in Oates' words, "life is a bungling process and in no way educational."[23]

Determined, however, to improve this depressing admission of life's absurdity, the filmmakers revised the closing scenes to stress the redemptive effect of love on the condemned man's soul. Now Frank listens sincerely to the priest, and he is made to agonize over being blamed for the death of Cora. As usual, Sackett shows up to say that he believes Frank innocent of killing Cora, but that he is being executed for killing Nick, as new evidence has been found linking Frank to that murder. This idea, inexplicably, makes Frank happy, even transcendant—suddenly convinced that Cora must understand his love, he faces death in hopes of a reunion with her. His face bathed in an almost mystical light, he looks up (heavenward?) with an awed, thankful expression. It seems that Cora's radiant whiteness, once a symbol of mysterious, compulsive evil, now represents her (or is it God's?) love and forgiveness. This is surely an incongruous note on which to end a film that has dealt, at least in intention, with a fateful conflict of passion, ambition, doom and entrapment. Sadly enough, by the end of the film, such bungling comes as no surprise. Although critics Madden and Van Nostrand describe it as a faithful (Madden claims almost literal) adaptation of the novel, the film version of *Postman* is really only intermittently related to Cain's vision and remains consistently uncertain of its own logic; ultimately it betrays all its assets of casting and story in a disastrous attempt to reconcile an existential drama with the world of reason and hope which it inherently denies.

4

MARATHON MAN/
MARATHON WOMAN

THE NOVEL
They Shoot Horses, Don't They?
(1935, Horace McCoy)

THE FILM
They Shoot Horses, Don't They?
(1969, Sydney Pollack)

Despite the highly favorable reviews that greeted its publication, Horace McCoy's *They Shoot Horses, Don't They?* (1935) has inspired much more lasting enthusiasm within the Hollywood community that had supplied its setting than among the American critical establishment[1] or the general reading public. Over the years, various filmmakers (Chaplin among them) discussed the possibility of adaptation, and the popular version that Sydney Pollack directed in 1969 at last assured McCoy of a wider recognition than he had ever managed to achieve in this country as a mere literary figure.

In Europe, on the other hand, particularly among the French, he has long enjoyed both a substantial reputation and the continuing popularity of frequent reissuance in new editions and translations of all his works. Some forty years ago, *They Shoot Horses* (in the American and English editions) created an underground sensation in France, even though it was not to be published in translation (as *On Acheve Bien les Chevaux*) until 1946, eleven years after its appearance in the U.S. By the late forties the Paris intellectual community had identified "a curious trinity: Hemingway, Faulkner, and McCoy,"[2] and the *New York Herald Tribune* even described McCoy as "the most discussed American writer in France."[3] Paul Nathan reported on this sensational "vogue":

> According to Mr. McCoy, the reason the French like him so much is that he is the real founder of existentialism—a philosophy which was labeled thus by his followers—and he claims to have letters from Sartre and others of his school to prove it.[4]

Regardless of the accuracy of this claim, McCoy had clearly struck a responsive chord among the continental avant-garde and had found his most enthusiastic audience far from his native milieu of the American Southwest.

McCoy, formerly a journalist working on various Dallas newspapers and a sometime actor with the Dallas Little Theatre, emigrated in 1931 to Hollywood, where he joined the ranks and "shared the hardships, disappointments, and anxieties common to the 20,000 extras reportedly out of work."[5] (Both *They Shoot Horses* and the subsequent *I Should Have Stayed Home* reflect his firsthand experience of this underside of the Hollywood culture.) Within a few years, however, he had married a wealthy woman and was working as a scenarist at Columbia Studios. During this time he had also been writing—quite a number of his stories appeared in *Black Mask* magazine between 1927 and 1935—and mulling over an idea he had for a story about a marathon dance (*Dance Marathon* was an early title for the project). Having, without success, recommended it to Universal as a film subject, he turned out several preliminary versions in short story form.[6] Once, while working it into a novel, "he watched a dance then being staged on the Santa Monica Pier . . . and came away deeply disturbed by the bestiality of the spectacle."[7] Finally, in 1935, his long-held vision was published as *They Shoot Horses, Don't They?*

Four other novels followed, but in spite of the rage he had inspired in France, McCoy's reputation in America fell into a curious kind of limbo. Edmund Wilson included him among "the Boys in the Back Room," giving rise to some mistaken assumptions about the nature of his work that have unfairly hindered its consideration to the present day. Most damaging has been the impression that *They Shoot Horses* was apparently derived from James M. Cain's *The Postman Always Rings Twice*, although McCoy had clearly been evolving his story long before Cain's novel was published in 1934. McCoy himself complained in 1948 about the "obligatory" comparison to Cain and, in a letter to his paperback publisher, wrote, "I do not care for Cain's work, although there may be much he can teach me. I know this though— continued labeling of me as of 'the Cain School' (whatever the hell that is) and I shall slit either his throat or mine."[8]

If McCoy belonged to any school, it was more likely that of the "hard-boiled" writers of *Black Mask*. His early experience in that magazine genre combined with his background as a newspaperman to produce the characteristic objective technique which one critic claims was brought "to its furthest development" in his fourth novel, *Kiss Tomorrow Goodbye* (1948).[9] But McCoy was more than a hard-boiled novelist, and his work, like that of any good writer, resists easy categorization. *They Shoot Horses* has no real "tough-guy hero," and although the plot deals with "murder," it is not a mystery. McCoy's subject, rather, is the existential awareness of a hopeless conflict between the world and the individual self, and his portrait of the painful dilemma created by such conflict reveals an intensity of vision that raises it above any mere formula fiction.

They Shoot Horses is narrated in the first person by Robert Syverten, a young man just convicted of murder, as he stands before the judge who is sentencing him to death. In a series of flashbacks, he recalls his meeting with a defeated and cynical young woman, Gloria Beatty, and the series of events that led to the shooting for which he is being condemned. Like him, a Hollywood extra out of work, Gloria sees a chance to win some money in a dance marathon to be held at a California ocean-front amusement park and she convinces Robert to be her partner. An orphan and the victim of a hard life, Gloria has once attempted suicide and claims that she would again if she "had the guts." Robert, on the other hand, is a good-natured, rather naive young man who dreams of becoming a great director, but during the course of this short novel, his simple, unreflective optimism will be thoroughly undermined by Gloria's outbursts about the sordid and absurd nature of life and the futility of the marathon dance itself. Together they encounter increasing pain and disillusionment as the contest proceeds, until suddenly it is stopped, closed down because of a violent outbreak among the spectators.

Now utterly exhausted and sick of her meaningless existence—"I'm just a misfit," she says, "I haven't got anything to give to anybody"[10]—Gloria asks Robert to shoot her, and he, by this time glumly attuned to her fatalistic philosophy, is reminded of an incident from his childhood, when his grandfather mercifully killed an injured mare. Later, when the arresting policeman asks why he has shot Gloria, Robert replies, "They shoot horses, don't they?"

The plot seems melodramatic in summary, but McCoy manages to invest the story with unusual artistic depth by his skillful handling of the narrative. Robert Syverten's memories emerge in thirteen short chapters or fast-moving scenes, some of which take place in the past and some in the present. Each chapter is preceded by a fragment of the judge's sentence; the final page bears the phrase "May God have mercy on your soul." This interlacery technique poses an ironic contrast, basic to the novel's theme, between the legal facts of the case and the metaphysical, existential aspect of the "murderer's act." Robert's brief but vivid recollections then highlight the desperate sense of spiritual dislocation and fragmentation that underlies his and Gloria's mood of despair.

The novel exhibits a circular movement like that of the marathon dance itself: the narrative shifts from the on-going trial scene to various incidents in the couple's relationship, and occasionally to a more distant past (Robert's childhood), yet each separate episode takes on the immediacy of present action. His ability to move the reader in and out of these various time frames without interrupting the flow of the storytelling is McCoy's premier stylistic achievement in the novel, made possible, in part, by rendering all the memory and interior thought passages (which are printed in italics) in terse, straightforward prose. And, more important, he concentrates interest on Robert not as narrator but as participant in the action, providing thus a complex perspective on his characters' shared experience. Thomas Sturak comments, "In creating a first-person narrator who is at once outside and inside the story, McCoy is able to command, direct and, in this case, literally frame the reader's attention."[11]

It is Gloria Beatty, however, not Robert, who is the moving force in the novel's action and the mouthpiece for McCoy's vision of an absurd universe. Gloria is, in fact, in Sturak's words, "at once the dramatic matrix of the narrative and the embodiment of the novel's main theme."[12] Preoccupied with thoughts of suicide and her notion that life is a cruel and meaningless series of events, she projects an intensity of suffering that colors her every word. When Robert first meets her and suggests sitting in the park, she says, "Let's go sit and hate a bunch of people" (p. 20); later she remarks, "My old man got killed in the war in France. I wish I could get killed in a war" (p. 23). During the marathon, when Robert complains about her constant kidding and points out that "I don't ever razz you," she replies, "You don't have to. I get razzed by an

expert. God razzes me" (p. 48). Gloria's personality, at
length, becomes a perfect objective correlative of the world of
the marathon dance, her wearying cycles of frustration
echoing the futility of all activity: "This whole business is a
merry-go-round," she says. "When we get out of here we're
right back where we started" (p. 76).

Gloria's troubles are only by implication connected with
the world of the Depression. McCoy has carefully suppressed
any reference to the society beyond the novel, for what he is
attempting is not a sociological tract but an embodiment of
the absurdist vision in the consciousness of a realistic
protagonist. Gloria's childhood was a sordid one—"When my
uncle was home he was always making passes at me and when
he was on the road my aunt and I were always fighting" (p.
22)—leaving her as much an orphan in spirit as in fact. Now,
unable to relate successfully to men, impoverished and
unemployed, she sees no hope of escaping her pain in life. "I
wish God would strike me dead," she says, and then,
impatient for an end, she asks Robert to "pinch hit for
God. . . . it's the only way to get me out of my misery" (p.
127). There is no grand martyrdom in this gesture, no
existential protest, only a conviction of the utter futility of
existence. She does not deny God, but declares the concept of
God equally as abstract/meaningless as her own life and her
own death. She is spiritually dead already; Robert only
relieves her of the suffering body.

Her obsession with death is not the only symptom of
Gloria's spiritual emptiness, for she reacts to other characters
with an equally cynical attitude. She advises a pregnant
woman in the marathon that she should have an abortion, and
when Robert protests, she retorts, "A hell of a lot you know
about it. You'd been better off if you'd never been born" (p.
29). Later she rejects her sponsor, a woman in the audience
(the embodiment of Nathanael West's crowd who came to
California to die) who represents a perverse humanity's ability
to gain sustenance from the spectacle of others' suffering, to

They Shoot Horses, Don't They?: Gloria (Jane Fonda), defying the marathon, the Depression and even death, carries the sailor (Red Buttons) across the finish line. (Also pictured: Bruce Dern and Bonnie Bedelia)

enjoy the marathon as proof that one's own lot is not so miserable as that of the poor grotesques on the dance floor. Gloria feels no compassion for such twisted sensibilities, but turns away in disgust: "My God can you feature that old lady? She's a nut about these things. They ought to charge her room rent. . . . I hope I never live to be that old" (p. 38).

She does, however, reach an emotional high point when a women's reform group come to try to close the marathon, letting out all her years of bitterness, frustration, and pent-up feelings in an attack on these enemies of the moment:

> "It's time somebody got women like you told. . . . and I'm just the baby to do it. You're the kind of bitches who sneak in the toilet to read dirty books and tell filthy stories and then go out and try to spoil somebody else's fun. . . ."
> "Your Morals League and your goddam women's clubs. . . . filled with meddlesome old bitches who haven't had a lay in twenty years. Why don't you old dames go out and buy a lay once in a while? That's all that's wrong with you . . .". (p. 94)

At the end of her tirade she breaks down and cries, for the first time displaying an emotion other than anger:

> She slowly leaned forward in the chair, bending double, shaking and twitching with emotion, as if she had completely lost control of the upper half of her body. For a full moment the only sounds in the room were her sobs and the rise and fall of the ocean which came through the half-raised window. (p. 95)

McCoy brings together in this scene all aspects of the universe that have operated on Gloria—the amoral environment (her speech indicates her contention that morality is relative), the dance hall (institutionalized absurdity), and the waves (a recurrent symbol of the meaningless motion of existence). These combined forces have leveled Gloria, reducing her to a one-dimensional character and then to a lump of despair. The next time the waves beat against the shore she will be dead.

Robert's narration of the story, addressed to himself (he doesn't appear to say anything to the courtroom), demonstrates that, like Camus's Meursault, he is really no criminal. In the first chapter he explains:

> The Prosecuting Attorney was wrong when he told the jury she died in agony, friendless, alone except for her brutal murderer, out there on that black night on the edge of the Pacific. He was wrong as a man can be. She did not die in agony. She was relaxed and comfortable and she was smiling. It was the first time I had ever seen her smile. How could she have been in agony then? And she wasn't friendless.
>
> I was her very best friend. I was her only friend. So how could she have been friendless? (p. 11)

Just as his retelling of the story reveals why he killed Gloria, his interior monologues gradually demonstrate why he chooses not to defend himself.

At first Robert is represented as an innocent and a dreamer who longs to become a great Hollywood director. He is in love with nature, responding with delight to the motion of the sea and constantly wishing to dance in the sunlight. His careless view of life is dramatically counterbalanced and ultimately overturned by Gloria's stark pessimism. At one point in the novel he says to her, "You're the gloomiest person I've ever met." Later, in one of his monologues, he registers a changed sensitivity to her personality:

> All day Gloria had been very morbid. I asked her a hundred times what she was thinking about. "Nothing," she would reply. *I realize now how stupid I was. I should have known what she was thinking. Now that I look back on that last night I don't see how I possibly could have been so stupid. But in those days I was dumb about a lot of things.* (p. 111)

Dislocated like Gloria from life by his experience of her despair, Robert realizes that he cannot explain to the judge what he has learned and so cannot hope that his action will be understood. The very existence of the law assumes a rational universe in which justice can operate, in which there is some cause and effect; knowing now that there is no reason and no justice, Robert elects to remain silent. Just as Gloria once ruminated on "nothingness," so he will now say nothing. The novel concludes ironically with the judge's hope that God will have mercy on the condemned soul, a conventional and formulaic expression that has by this time been thoroughly undermined by Robert's growing awareness that God in fact shows no more mercy than the indifferent waves beating against the shore.

The novel achieves, despite its subject, a consistently detached and objective tone—McCoy's distinctive understated style. Sturak's analysis is apropos:

> . . . the uniqueness and force of this book are in part due to the fact that the actualities of Hollywood and of a marathon dance are to begin with bizarre. However, because McCoy exercises such controlled and dispassionate objectivity, we are satisfied that these things could not have happened otherwise, given what we learn about the characters; and we recognize that their implicit meanings transcend the narrative.[13]

As a grim and unyielding portrait of hopelessness, *They Shoot Horses, Don't They?* has few parallels in American literature. Its spare, detached style, perfectly matched with its claustrophobic content, embodies the modern, absurdist sensibility in an enduring image of spiritual despair.

In his review of the film, John Simon concluded that ". . . although *They Shoot Horses, Don't They?* does not, as a whole, reach the domain of art, many of its aspects and an aura that lingers on establish it as a true and eminent cinematic achievement."[14] This is a fair assessment, for despite some considerable flaws, the film remains an admirable achievement in the adaptation of a fictional theme.

Lean and spare in construction and presentation, McCoy's novel did not develop three-dimensional characters or clearly realistic social settings, but relied instead upon a kind of atmospheric incarnation of existential ideas. Even Gloria, its most roundly "developed" character, is too obsessed, too much an abstraction (in the tradition of the classic American novel), to convey any impression of flesh-and-blood reality. Recognizing the difficulty of transferring such intellectually conceptualized figures to the screen, director Sydney Pollack was forced to "flesh out" McCoy's vision, as he explained in the preface to the published version of the screenplay:

> When a film maker stands a person on the screen, that character has breadth and depth simply by virtue of being seen, and those dimensions must be filled in with action and dialogue in order for the character not to seem hollow. So some invention was needed to make the characters fully three-dimensional without violating the spare, simple flavor which McCoy intended and which does contribute so much to the work's success.[15]

This remark is significant as a frank admission of the conflict of values that makes of Pollack's film such an interesting combination of success and failure in the moviemaker's art of "invention." Skillfully filling in the gaps of experience and motivation in McCoy's characters, he renders them believable and recognizably human, managing thus to expand and clarify the absurd landscape of the dance marathon. Unfortunately, however, his determination to remain faithful to the "spare, simple flavor" of McCoy's narrative works against this effort of realism, producing at once a splendid depiction of the world of the marathon and a strangely muddled philosophic statement.

The film's main problem is in its depiction of Gloria. Despite the frizzled hair and makeup, Jane Fonda remains too attractive for the role of chronic loser, the woman described in the novel as one who "with a nice wardrobe might have looked attractive, but even then I wouldn't have called her pretty." In Fonda's presence, it is simply hard to swallow Gloria's contention that she is unsuccessful with men. Worse than this (perhaps unavoidable) physical discrepancy, however, is the corresponding prettification of her personality. In giving texture and depth to Gloria's characterization, the screenwriters (James Poe and Robert E. Thompson[16]) have made her too nice and too resourceful. This Gloria is too obviously a survivor to fall prey to the existential despair required to establish her final death-wish, and although she shares something of her fictional counterpart's hard-boiled attitude, she cannot match the ferocity and conviction of McCoy's utterly defeated protagonist.

She is introduced as she waits in line to enter the marathon. The world of the film is wholly bounded by the marathon, and McCoy's preliminary scenes of Gloria and Robert's meeting in Los Angeles have been relocated almost entirely inside the dance hall.

Her first remarks, in an exchange with a sailor (Red Buttons), a character created for the film, are reminiscent of the Gloria of the novel:

> SAILOR: . . . Once between hitches I worked a cattle boat out'a Galveston. Same thing. Know what I mean?. . . . I mean if you think about it, cattle ain't got it much worse than us.
> GLORIA'S VOICE: They got it better. There's always somebody to feed 'em. . . .
>
> SAILOR: Yeah sure . . . stuffin' 'em up good for the slaughter pen. Right down a chute, and some big dumb bohunk's standin' there with a sledgehammer. . . .
> GLORIA: They don't know its gonna happen. That makes 'em one up on us, don't it?[17]

This cynical posture is not sustained, however, for during the marathon she will become attracted to Robert and her attitude will increasingly soften with the attachment. Fonda's performance indicates that Gloria's tough stance is really a pose, more a defense mechanism than a deep-rooted expression of her personality. When the husband (Bruce Dern) of Ruby, the pregnant dancer (Bonnie Bedelia), attempts to punch Gloria for bothering his wife about the baby, Robert (Michael Sarrazin) steps in to protect her, and she is clearly touched. And, though she continually tells Ruby to have an abortion ("Why drop . . . another sucker into this mess?"), Fonda's facial expressions suggest that she doesn't really mean what she is saying, that beneath the hard exterior she really longs for the values of home and family which the baby represents. Later, when she discovers that Robert has had sex with Alice (Susannah York), an actress who is trying to get discovered at the marathon, she reacts with the outrage born of jealousy, refusing to stay partners with him until she is forced to do so. Such vulnerability to emotional attachment makes her a very sympathetic character, unlike the hard-boiled Gloria of the novel, who could not have formed any real attachment to Robert and would certainly never have cared about his sexual liaisons.

Fonda's Gloria is also determined to win the marathon, and the vitality of her exertions creates some confusion about the state of her mind. During one of the races around the dance floor (a device used to spice up the proceedings when attendance lags), Gloria, screaming "Walk, you son of a bitch," carries the corpse of the sailor on her back—defying the marathon, the Depression, even life itself, in her desire to get to the finish line. This is not the action of someone who is down on life and wants to die; this character displays too much strength and determination to lead up convincingly to the death-wish that climaxes her experience. When this Gloria at last asks Robert to shoot her, there seems too little reason for her sudden despair, too little motivation for such acceptance of defeat.

Apparently recognizing this inconsistency, the screenwriters invented several incidents to explain Gloria's ultimate sense of defeat, but they only manage thus to trivialize the effect of her despair. Her painful discovery that Robert has, in a sense, been "unfaithful" to her is followed by the even more devastating realization that the marathon itself is a cheat. Rocky, the emcee, suggests that Gloria and Robert marry on the dance floor, and when she refuses, he explains that he is trying to do her a favor, that she can hock the gifts and make a couple of hundred dollars out of it. Even if she were to win the marathon, he adds, he would have to deduct expenses:

> "What the hell do you think it cost me for those track suits?—and the new shoes—all the extra meals?—your laundry bills—newspapers, magazines?—I mean, it all adds up— Naturally, you don't win you don't pay. I'm not out to cheat anybody." (p. 308)

To which Gloria replies, "It's all for nothing!" She then decides to quit the marathon, realizing the futility of it. The last straw comes when Robert accidently rips one of her stockings, her last pair and something she "cut out streetcars for a month" to buy. She breaks down and cries (for the first time in the film), then walks out onto the pier with Robert and asks him to shoot her. Somehow the sum of the provocations exhibited here does not seem enough to drive this woman, the Gloria created by Fonda and the screenwriters—so resourceful, so determined and emotionally involved—to commit suicide. Once partnered with a corpse and yet defiant, she suddenly abandons all hope over a torn stocking and the loss of some prize money—too swiftly defeated by symbolic trifles, she makes an unconvincing victim of existential anguish.

The portrayal of Robert is even less effective in the film. Having wisely dropped the interior monologues which reveal Robert's growing awareness in the novel, Pollack and his screenwriters do not manage to create any substitute means of character development suitable for the film medium. Consequently this major figure remains vague, and Michael Sarrazin's unfocused performance fails to provide any depth or emotional life. Unlike McCoy's Robert, who demonstrates an increasing understanding and sympathy for Gloria's plight, the Robert of the film appears consistently naive and confused throughout the story and seems unaffected by her suffering and cynicism. Finally, his motive for entering upon the death pact with Gloria is as unclear and unconvincing as her death-wish itself.

Unable, despite his expressed desire to do so, to remain faithful to McCoy's vision, Pollack instead devotes his film to an exploration of the emptiness of the American dream and the corrupt economic system that underlies it. Carrying the main thematic weight in this revised concept is a character almost wholly created by the screenwriters, Rocky the emcee—little more than a name in the novel, he is the most fully realized character in the film (and played to the hilt by Gig Young, in the film's finest performance). A smooth, fast-talking salesman who knows how to take advantage of his audience's weakness, he sells his product, the marathon, by appealing to the desperate need for excitement that draws them to the spectacle.

Variously grotesque in their yearning for such entertainment—the film's evocation of their twisted sensibilities is keyed on Madge Kennedy's well-conceived, though brief, portrayal of Mrs. Layden, Gloria's sponsor—these spectators have come to the dance marathon seeking some thrill, which is missing from their dull, poverty-stricken lives. They are the masses who came to Southern California in pursuit of its promise of happiness, only to find that the Depression has followed them there and so the promise has proven false; Nathanael West describes them best in *The Day of the Locust:*

> Once there, they discover that sunshine isn't enough. They get tired of oranges, even of avocado pears and passion fruit.

Nothing happens. They don't know what to do with their time. They haven't the mental equipment for leisure, the money nor the physical equipment for pleasure. What else is there? . . . If only a plane would crash once in a while so that they could watch the passengers being consumed in a "holocaust of flame," as the newspapers put it. But the planes never crash.[18]

This is Rocky's audience, his clientele—he feeds their shallow dreams by using the language of advertising promotion which has degraded the language as well as the dream. When the sailor has done a sad soft-shoe dance for pennies from the audience, Rocky exploits the moment with a glib appeal to cheap sentimentality:

You can all see that Harry used to be in the U.S. Navy. . . . but there's something you can't see. I want to be serious for a moment, folks, if you'll permit me. Harry Klein is one of those brave young men who went sailing off to beat the Kaiser. That's right, a veteran of the Great War. . . . and let's hope there'll never be another. Harry was decorated in that War . . . for wounds received in action. But that's not all. . . . I know Harry wouldn't want me to tell you this, but RIGHT NOW . . . at THIS MOMENT, there are thirty-two separate pieces of shrapnel still embedded in Harry's body. And here he is, fighting another kind of war, fighting to win. . . . Isn't that the grit and never say die spirit that made this the great country it is? (pp. 165-66)

Rocky perfectly understands his business and his audience. The son of a faith healer, he learned as a child how gullible people are and how to manipulate them. The villain of the piece, he knows the unhappiness of life and sees the falsity of the dream, yet he perpetuates the lie and debases the unhappiness itself by playing upon his customers' perverse delight in the spectacle of suffering. Late in the film he explains to Robert why he stole the glamorous dress of one of the contestants:

ROBERT: It's a contest. Isn't that what it's supposed to be?
ROCKY: Not for them. For you, maybe. But not for them. You
think they're laying out two bits a throw just to watch you
poke your head up into the sunlight? or Alice look like she just
stepped out of a beauty parlor? They don't care whether you
win! . . . They want to see a little misery out there so they
can feel a little better maybe. They're entitled to that. (pp.
247-49)

In another scene a contestant breaks down emotionally in the
rest area and Rocky calms her down; when Gloria sarcastically
comments, "I'm surprised you didn't put her on display.
Charge a little extra." Rocky only answers, "No. It's too
real."—his showmanship is clearly based on a shrewd and
utterly unfeeling sense of life's inadequacy to the purposes of
the spectacle.

Despite his cynicism and salesman's sleaziness, Rocky
does have a certain hard-boiled charm, and Gig Young's
performance nicely balances the two aspects of the character.
(John Simon declared that "Young has just the right good looks
gone partly to seed, and the properly flexible voice that turns
oily in the limelight and greedy in the shadows."[19]) Unfortunately, again, this amelioration of personality tends to
undermine the film's attack on the fakery behind the American dream, as represented in Rocky's relentless tactics of
exploitation. As in the case of Gloria, the filmmakers sacrifice
much of their story's force and thematic unity by confounding
contradictory impulses in a character whose role is clearly
symbolic.[20]

The film succeeds, nevertheless, in presenting a fine
study of the American dream cheat and its archetypal
exploiter, and it manages, in addition, to bring vividly to life
the world of the marathon dance. Pollack focuses continually
on the contestants, revealing their pain and their determination as they support one another in exhaustion on the dance
floor or retire to the rest area (not described in the novel),
where they wash, sleep, or stuff toilet paper in their shoes.

Philip Lathrop's color photography contributes alternately a garish macabre quality and an understated, shoddy look which enhances the film's thematic statement. One of Pollack's most effective techniques involves his handling of the grueling foot races which occasionally interrupt the dancing in order to excite the customers' interest and eliminate some contestants—sometimes in quick cuts, sometimes in slow motion, he focuses on the strained faces and bodies of the racers, emphasizing the brutality of the spectacle (and, by implication, of the American system) and the desperation of its victims.

Pollack realized that the marathon was indeed his theme, and he reshaped the story's ending in order to reinforce it. Whereas McCoy ended the novel with the closing of the marathon, Gloria's death, and the pronouncement of Robert's death sentence, Pollack replaces this theatricality with a simple reassertion of the scene: after Robert shoots Gloria, the camera returns to the marathon and we hear Rocky's voice droning on, ". . . while the clock of fate ticks away. While the dance of destiny continues. While the marathon goes on and on and on. . . ." Gloria's defeat and death are absorbed into the motion of the marathon; rather than the finality and crushing doom of McCoy's ending, Pollack's vision dissolves upon an image of the ongoing struggle of survival.

The film's achievements are solid ones: the sordid and grotesque world of the marathon—the distorted characters who inhabit that world, and the marathon itself as a symbol of human degradation—are in many ways more forcefully portrayed in the film than in the novel. Pollack rightly decided to flesh out McCoy's narrative, which, very much a literary *tour de force,* could not have been successfully transferred to the screen without major alterations. The film's increased development of setting and character serves to expand upon the novel's central image. However, in trying to remain too faithful to McCoy's vision rather than to his own, Pollack pulled his film in opposite directions, confusing its thematic focus and undermining the credibility of two of its central characters. Imaginatively conceived and vividly realized in its parts, his version is incompletely integrated and so never achieves the dramatic intensity that inspires McCoy's novel.

5

THE WAGES OF SIN

THE NOVEL
The Treasure of the Sierra Madre
(1927, 1935, B. Traven)

THE FILM
The Treasure of the Sierra Madre
(1948, John Huston)

John Huston, screenwriter and director of *The Treasure of the Sierra Madre* (1948), has devoted much of his career to transfering important literary works to the screen. Beginning with Dashiell Hammett's *The Maltese Falcon* (1941) and Ellen Glasgow's *In This Our Life* (1942), Huston went on to direct adaptations of, in addition to B. Traven's novel, Stephen Crane's *The Red Badge of Courage* (1951), Herman Melville's *Moby Dick* (1956), Tennessee Williams' *The Night of the Iguana* (1964), Carson McCullers' *Reflections in a Golden Eye* (1967), and Rudyard Kipling's *The Man Who Would be King* (1975), even tackling the Bible in 1966. Certainly Huston is a first-rate craftsman, possessing a profound knowledge of film structure and pacing, but he is not an intellectual director, and many of his screen versions lack the thematic complexity and texture of the originals.

The simplifying influence of Huston's directorial (and authorial) influence is clearly evident in two of his most highly regarded adaptations, *Moby Dick* and *Sierra Madre*. The two novels themselves are, in fact, comparable not on the basis of artistic achievement, but on the basis of structure: each is organized around a quest, which is to prove futile—a basic archetypal pattern whose mythic, historical, and psychological reverberations are mined for the enrichment of the surface narrative. Both novelists frequently digress from their plots to offer lengthy asides designed to consolidate their works' metaphysical premises, Melville's expository chapters on the commercial and industrial aspects of whaling and his philosophical speculations on the nature of good and evil corresponding to Traven's discourses on the subject of gold, Catholicism, and the Indian culture. Both novels thus are more than mere adventure stories, in effect presenting exhaustive studies of the physical and moral lore of their subject-settings, their times, and the human societies in which their tales are set. Confronting, then, the need imposed by the film medium, for the visual interpretation and condensation of such elaborate fictional constructs, Huston, in both cases, boldly cuts the novels loose from their philosophic moorings and emphasizes instead the adventure-narrative qualities of their central plot sequences; what metaphysical texture he does retain is considerably simplified. In her analysis of the film version of *Moby Dick*, Brandon French writes that "the universe in the Huston-Bradbury production of *Moby Dick* has firm moral polarities"—gone is Melville's "adventure of the human soul in a chaotic universe of indeterminate morality."[1] The same is true of *Sierra Madre*, whose universe, too, has been suddenly stabilized, its characters made into obvious exemplars of stages of moral development. Traven's universe, like Melville's, is one of "indeterminate morality"; Huston's is not.

Like Melville, Traven was a wanderer. His mysterious life and hidden identity have fascinated his critics, almost to the neglect of his writings themselves. During his lifetime Traven insisted on anonymity and pursued it with an almost maniacal intensity. Under the name of Hal Croves, supposedly Traven's agent, he told Judy Stone, "Forget the man! What does it matter if he is the son of a Hohenzollern prince or anyone else? Write about his work."[2] Another time, he handed a reporter a copy of his "Declaration of Independence from Personal Publicity," which reads in part:

> I simply do not understand why such a fuss is made about a writer, so that people want to know at what time he gets up, when he breakfasts, if he drinks, smokes, eats meat, if he plays golf or poker, if he is married or single. My work is important, I am not; I am only a common, ordinary worker. The god of nature granted me the gift of writing books, therefore I am obliged to write books instead of baking bread.[3]

Nevertheless, the thrust of most of the material on Traven has been in pursuit of the man, not of "the works."

The story of this man's life remains still somewhat hypothetical, but most of his critics present certain "facts" consistently: he was born Traven Torsvan Croves in Chicago on May 3, 1890, the son of Scandinavian immigrants, although the Registry of Foreigners in Mexico for 1930 lists a man named Berick Traven Torsvan from Chicago as having immigrated to that country. Traven has also been linked with the German actor and anti-war anarchist, Ret Marut, as many of his books, originally published in German, display a style and philosophy similar to Marut's. Little is known about Marut, who clung to his anonymity as determinedly as Traven, declaring:

> I shall always and at all times prefer to be pissed on by dogs and it will appear to me to be a greater honor than to be pissed on by readers of *Der Ziegelbrenner* [his newspaper] with letters that

attempt to sniff out holes in my garment in order to pin me
down, for no one else has the opportunity of boring himself into
my flesh.[4]

What is known of him is that between 1907 and 1915, Marut
was a stage actor, speaking German with a "a slight accent and
English."[5] He quit acting in 1915 and moved to Munich, and
on September 1, 1917, brought out the first issue of *Der
Ziegelbrenner*, a paper that condemned war and nationalism.
(One theory as to Marut's ability to finance the paper was that
he was the illegitimate son of Kaiser Wilhelm II.) He
participated in the establishment of the short-lived Munich
Raterepublik in 1919 and was arrested shortly thereafter. He
was to be shot but managed to escape and finally to leave
Germany in 1922. The mystery of his identity is compounded
by Marut's police registration card, which states that he was
born in San Francisco on February 25, 1882. Michael
Baumann, however, through extensive comparisons of style
and ideas in Marut/Traven's German writings, concludes that
"B. Traven had once been Ret Marut."[6] One of his pieces of
evidence is that after his disappearance from Germany in
1922, Marut appeared in Mexico a year later, and the likely
consolidation of the two identities at least supports Baumann's
contention that Traven was an American writer, as Traven
himself always insisted he was.

In 1946, John Huston began writing letters to Traven
about the proposed film of *Sierra Madre* and received in reply
long letters containing suggestions. Huston requested an
interview, but instead of Traven, was met by "Hal Croves,"
who brought a letter from Traven which explained that he
(Traven) would be unable to meet Huston but that "Croves
knew Traven's work better than I do." [7] Huston hired Croves
as a technical advisor and eventually guessed that Croves and
Traven were the same person. Rumors spread on the set,
angrily denounced by Croves, who then began making
outrageous suggestions about the film, among them that

Walter Huston was not right for the role of Howard and should be replaced. (For his performance, of course, Huston was to win an Academy Award as Best Supporting Actor.)

Traven/Croves lived in Mexico until his death on March 26, 1969. His widow, Rosa Elena Lujan, discussing his will, revealed that in that document Traven had finally cleared up the mystery of his identity:

> She said that Traven Torsvan was his real name, that he was born in Chicago, Illinois, on May 3, 1890, the son of Burton Torsvan, a Norwegian farmer, and Dorothy Croves, an English-woman who soon tired of America and settled in Germany. Later he used the *noms de plume* of B. Traven, Ret Marut and Hal Croves.[8]

Other biographical information about Traven can be inferred from the novels in which his fictional persona, Gerald Gales, appears. In one of his finest books, *The Death Ship* (published in Germany in 1926 and here in 1934), a sea novel probably about Traven's own withdrawal from America and Europe, the link with Melville is further pronounced in descriptions of life and work aboard a ship and in narrative preoccupations with death and the loss of identity. Gales even calls himself "Pippip," openly establishing connections with Melville's Pip—and, perhaps, Dickens'?—who discovers the secret of the deep (man's anonymous and absurd existence) and concludes that he no longer really belongs among the living. Traven's other major novel in which Gales appears is *The Bridge in the Jungle* (published in Germany in 1929 and in America in 1938; in a 1971 Mexican film version directed by Pancho Kohner, John Huston appears as Sleigh), wherein Gales is the narrator, not the protagonist, of another tale about death and rebirth.

Traven's major fiction is very much preoccupied with the themes of death and the discovery or disintegration of the self, regularly employing the archetypal structure of the descent into self or the process of losing oneself in order to discover the self. There are, of course, shades of Conrad here, too, and the influence is marked, especially in Traven's concern with the symbolic journey and the individual personality tested beyond the boundaries of civilized society. *The Treasure of the Sierra Madre* clearly follows this pattern: in it three down-and-out Americans in Mexico leave society behind to go prospecting for gold in the Sierra Madre—the mountains of the mother. Stripped of all civilizing restraints, they descend into the earth/womb, intending, in a sense, to rob the mother of her golden treasure. The effect of this quest on the characters of the three men varies with each individual's ability to learn from experience and to perceive what the real treasure is. Traven's epigraph to the novel provides an enigmatic précis of the knowledge to be gained:

> The treasure which you think not worth taking trouble and pains to find, this one alone is the real treasure you are longing for all your life. The glittering treasure you are hunting for day and night lies buried on the other side of that hill yonder.

The novel opens in Tampico, a poverty-stricken town that serves as a gathering place for lost, superfluous souls. Traven's chief protagonist, Fred C. Dobbs, is introduced immediately as a man who has "less than nothing"—like one of the marginal men on the Death Ship, he is ready for a voyage out. The place is described as a kind of no-exit hell, which one can escape only by railway, and few have the money for a ticket: "There were no roads on which cars could run . . . the port was protected on one side by the sea, on the other side by rivers, swamps and jungle."[9] Even nature offers no solace, as is made clear when Dobbs goes to bathe in a river:

> Here in the river bathing was not all pleasure. The river-bottom was muddy and infested with horseshoe crabs. Any foot which invaded their dwellings was badly treated by those giant crabs,

and many a bather feared that he might go home one toe short. (p. 23)

Most of the people here are too poor to afford even a room; the more fortunate stay at the Hotel Oso Negro, an airless, broken-down place, almost unreal and barely standing. Those who make use of its dingy shelter are nameless— . . . information concerning a patron, his nationality, his profession, his home town, was of no interest to the clerk or to the police" (p. 18). The phantom nature of the place, its graveyard quality, is emphasized in the reference to a shelf where "dead letters" (another Melvillean reference) are kept:

A shelf with little compartments was filled with letters for patrons. Bundles of letters, many of them from a mother, a wife, or a sweetheart, were piled up, covered with thick dust. The men to whom they were addressed might be dead, or working deep in the jungles, clearing new oil-fields, or on a tramp in the China Sea. . . . (p. 18)

Traven's Tampico, thus, becomes a realized picture of the state of Bartleby's soul—Melville writes: "Dead letters! Does it not sound like dead men?"

Because Dobbs is able to beg some money, he can afford to stay at the hotel. Traven's description of him is significant: "Dobbs had no suitcase with him, not even a pasteboard box or a paper bag. He would not have known what to put into them. All he possessed in this world he carried in his pants pockets" (p. 14). This man, it seems, experiences life in the raw, at its cruelest, basest and most degraded; without the comforts necessary to cushion experience, he sees life stripped to the bone, exposed in its barbaric essence. In many ways he resembles Hannah Arendt's concentration camp inmates:

The concentration camp inmate has no price, because he can always be replaced; nobody knows to whom he belongs, because he is never seen. From the point of view of normal society he is

absolutely superfluous, although in times of acute labor short-
age, as in Russia and in Germany during the war, he is used for
work. [10]

But it is difficult for Dobbs even to find work. He and a friend
named Moulton make a treacherous trip through the jungle to
look for work in the oil-fields, another hell where man has
even "improved" on nature: "The air bit into your lungs
because it was filled with poisonous gas escaping from the
refineries. The sting in the air which made breathing so hard
and unpleasant and choked your throat constantly meant that
people were making money—much money" (pp. 27–28). Still,
there is no work, and the two men return to Tampico.

Shortly afterward Dobbs does find a job with a contractor
named Pat McCormick, setting up an oil-camp. The conditions are brutal and the pay meager—Dobbs has only entered
another circle of hell:

> The heat was never less than one hundred degrees in the open,
> where all the work had to be done surrounded by jungle. He
> was pestered by the ten thousand sorts of insects and reptiles
> the jungle breeds. He thought a hundred times a day that his
> eyes would burn away from the heat above and around him. (pp.
> 46–47)

When, after all this, McCormick does not pay the men,
Dobbs teams up with Curtin, who will later join him on the
expedition to the Sierra Madre, and they search out McCormick and get their money.

At the hotel Dobbs meets Howard, an old prospector full
of tales of gold prospecting. The idea of such an adventure
naturally seems attractive to a man with literally nothing to
lose, so Dobbs discusses it with Curtin, and they decide to set
out with Howard to look for gold. Dobbs sees the journey in
very pedestrian terms:

> Dobbs had never before in his life thought that prospecting for
> gold necessarily must carry some sort of mystery with it.

> Prospecting for gold was only another way of looking for a job or working. There was no more mystery about it than about digging out a tank on a cattle ranch or working in a sand mine. (p. 76)

He will, of course, learn otherwise, although that "mystery" is something he will never really understand.

Howard, in contrast, is an older and wiser man, who has been on many expeditions for gold and has absorbed many of the lessons of the journey. When introduced, he is lecturing a group of people about the evil effect of gold; like that of Chaucer's Pardoner, his theme is "radux malorum est cupiditas"[11] —on a superficial level this is Traven's theme as well:

> . . . Gold is a very devilish sort of thing, believe me, boys. In the first place, it changes your character entirely. When you have it your soul is no longer the same as it was before . . . You can no longer see clearly what is good and what is bad. You lose your judgment. . . .
>
> All the time murder's lurking about . . . worst of all, hardly a day passes without quarrels, everybody accusing everybody else of all sorts of crimes, and suspecting whatever you do or say or even look at. As long as there's no find, the noble brotherhood will last. Woe when the piles begin to grow! Then you know your men and what they are worth. (pp. 58, 60)

Howard will be the guide for Dobbs and Curtin as they begin their voyage into darkness, but Traven does not attempt to present him as morally pure or all-wise—he is no Virgil, and he, too, must learn from this journey.

Dobbs and Curtin become aware of how much they need Howard as soon as the expedition begins:

> Had they been alone, they would not have been able to follow even a trail. They had no idea how to keep the burros at the camp during the night, how to pack them the right way, or how to make them go over the rocky path across the high mountains,

where often the boys themselves could not get hold with their feet. (p. 84)

The men soon realize that prospecting for gold is a very difficult business—Dobbs thus encounters his third back-breaking situation, though now he is working for himself and has hopes of great reward. Traven is very American in his emphasis on men who leave civilization behind to look for opportunities in more open spaces, and his three prospectors certainly seem freer "on the road." Traven's "road," however, is not an easy one to walk, and the open spaces do not so certainly offer the promise of renewal.

Howard's warning about gold's ability to "change men's souls" is justified as soon as the men begin to accumulate some—the gold begins to separate them. They divide their proceeds every night, and each carefully hides his share from the others. United only by their greed, they now "had in common only their business relations." Howard alone is able to maintain some semblance of control during this difficult period. Traven refers to Dobbs and Curtin as "the two youngsters," whom Howard must keep from fighting: regressing toward brutishness under the pressure of their degraded sensibilities, they suggest the unruly forces of the id, warily kept in check by the more stable influence of the rational ego.

This uneasy little community is soon intruded upon by Lacaud, who also has come to the mountains in search of gold. Worried by his presence, Dobbs and Curtin want to kill him, but Howard opposes it, and so they agree to let Lacaud stay around and share in whatever profits are to be made. Their talk is interrupted by the approach of some bandits, and Traven temporarily suspends the action here to include an extended tale about the bandits, narrated by Lacaud.

This is the second of the novel's inset narratives, the first having evolved in Howard's lectures on the nature of gold. Describing the Spaniards' exploitation of *La Mina Agua* (Greenwater Mine) and their brutalization of the Indian workers, the Indians' revolt and massacre of the Spanish, and the resulting centuries-old curse that hangs over the mine, this first tale was designed to annunciate the central tenet of Howard's (and Traven's) cynical perceptions:

> Men, Christians and Jews alike, are so greedy or brave where gold is at stake that, regardless how many human beings it may cost, as long as the gold itself does not give out and disappear, they will risk life, health, and mind, and face every danger and risk conceivable, to get hold of the precious metal. (p. 63)

In addition, this early narrative served to inculcate an appreciation of Mexican history and of the role of the Catholic Church, the Spanish, and capitalist exploiters in perverting the agrarian, peaceful Mexican way of life.

Lacaud's tale, too, is full of Traven's editorializing, superimposed on a harsh account of these bandits robbing a train, torturing and murdering many of the passengers. The details are graphic and the level of violence mixes with Traven's earlier portraits of decay in presenting a corrosive portrait of man and society. (It should be pointed out that Traven is not a political writer, as he has often mistakenly been presented; he has no belief in isms, except perhaps anarchism, but seems to adhere to an idyllic vision of peaceful, isolated existence, wherein man remains in touch with land and family, insisting steadily that the growth of political communities only leads to chaos.) Lacaud's tale also provides material for further indictment of the Church, as the bandits pillage and murder in the name of Christ.

The final lengthy narrative is provided, again, by Howard and concerns the difficulty of the return journey—"Gold is of no use to anybody as long as it is not where he wants it." This, another tale of greed, the perversions of the Church, and murder, presents in contrast Traven's positive vision of the proper way of life. All-wise and in touch with the real principles of wealth, the native Mexicans practice a virtuous humanity best expressed later in the words of an Indian chief:

I do not need gold nor do I want silver. I have plenty to eat always. I have a young and beautiful wife, whom I love dearly and who loves and honors me. I have also a strong and healthy boy, who now, thanks to your skill, can see and so is perfect in every way. I have my acres and fields, and I have my fine cattle. I am chief and judge, and I may say I am a true and honest friend of my tribe, which respects me and obeys my orders, which they know are for their own good. . . .So what could gold mean to me? Gold and silver do not carry any blessing. . . .You whites, you kill and rob and cheat and betray for gold. You hate each other for gold, while you never can buy love with gold. Nothing but hatred and envy. You whites spoil the beauty of life for the possession of gold. (p. 203)

When the men are ready to leave the mountain, Howard again demonstrates his wisdom and respect for nature by insisting that they restore the mountain: "So we shouldn't leave this place as careless picnic parties and dirty motorists often do. We have wounded this mountain and I think it is our duty to close its wounds. The silent beauty of this place deserves our respect" (p. 189). Dobbs and Curtin are, of course, puzzled, but they agree.

On the way back to civilization (by now a thoroughly ironic concept), Howard revives an Indian boy suffering from shock and is forced to accept the Indians' hospitality. Placing his treasure in the keeping of Curtin and Dobbs, he promises to meet them in Durango. Curtin and Dobbs are thus left without Howard for the rest of the journey, and their partnership quickly disintegrates. They continually quarrel about who is to do what—"Now it seemed as if they had lost the capacity for sound and simple reasoning."

Earlier, even before Howard's departure, Dobbs' behavior has shown signs of change, causing Howard to remark, "You behave like a child." Now Dobbs entirely loses control of himself, regressing even further: "Unexpectedly Dobbs pushed Curtin in the ribs and laughed in a curious way." His greed asserts itself openly, as he implies that Howard was foolish to leave his gold with them. Curtin objects and defends his own nobler philosophy: "I may not respect many things in life, but I do respect most sincerely the money somebody has worked and slaved for honestly." Dobbs calls him a Bolshevik, adding, "a soap-box always makes me sick. And to have to hear it even out here in the wilderness is the god-damned limit." While his cynicism does serve effectively to temper the naïveté of a too-ready faith in human nature, Dobbs' animal rapacity is here doubly condemned in the contrast to Curtin's proletarian ethic. Accused by Dobbs of trying to cheat him, Curtin soon realizes the danger he is in: "He saw danger lurking, and he knew he could not elude it." (p. 248)

As Dobbs regresses further and further, Traven emphasizes his incipient bestiality—he is described as "squatting" and "crawling" and his laughter sounds like "barking." In another allusive passage, Dobbs says to Curtin that "I only want to free myself of you"—it is clear that, once freed of Howard and Curtin, his last link to civilized behavior, Dobbs could regress totally. Curtin realizes that he would have to kill Dobbs to get himself out of danger, but he can't do it: "In a situation like this, Dobbs was the stronger, because he would act upon impulse and think afterwards." And so he does; soon he is able to surprise Curtin and shoot him. Immediately his conscience bothers him—he feels cold even though he is lying beside a fire, and his laughter becomes unnatural. He vows "not to lose himself in that god-damned Sierra," but, unfortunately, he already has.

Significantly, when Dobbs leaves the mountain, he feels better:

> He knew his conscience would not trouble him here. Such things only happened in the mountains, where trees seemed to speak and foliage to frame strange faces. Here, in full view of the plain, he found real tranquillity. He sang and whistled as he cooked his meal. (p. 268)

This tranquillity is short-lived, however. Just as he comes in sight of town, Dobbs finds himself surrounded by three tramps, poor men who have been out of work for a long time (like Dobbs himself at the novel's opening). They kill Dobbs for his boots and burros and what they think are hides—chopping off his head, they really only confirm in physical terms the loss of reason that has already destroyed his humanity.

In dividing up Dobbs' possessions, the three bandits offer a striking parallel to the three gold-seekers at their worst, arguing and bickering over the spoils of their crime. As a crowning irony, these partners don't even recognize the gold for what it is, but mistake it for sand and pour it out: "Then came the night breeze which carried all the sand, strewn about the ground, far and wide in all directions" (p. 286). Traven, with his love of the earth, openly approves that quality of these men which, in ignorance of the "value" of the gold, return it to nature. However, like Dobbs, they are incomplete beings, and they, too, will die (they are later executed for their crime).

Meanwhile, Howard's reputation as a great healer and miracle worker has spread through the Indian villages in the mountains. Called one day to treat a wounded man, he recognizes him as Curtin, and nurses him back to health. When they learn from an Indian of the fate of Dobbs and their gold, Howard "let out such a roar of Homeric laughter that his companions thought him crazy," though in truth he displays his wisdom again in recognizing the absurdity of the whole episode and the fitness of its outcome:

> Anyway, I think it's a very good joke—a good one played on us and on the bandits by the Lord or by fate or by nature, whichever you prefer. And whoever or whatever played it certainly had a good sense of humor. The gold has gone back where we got it. (pp. 316–17)

Curtin soon sees the joke, too, and joins in the laughter. Soon thereafter, however, they learn that two bags of gold have been recovered, and so the two consider the possibility of using the money to go into business together. Finally they reject this plan; Howard decides to stay with the Indians as their doctor and Curtin says he will join him when he recovers from his wounds.

Traven's adventure tale of a search for gold is also, then, an archetypal tale of the search for the self, as Dobbs, Curtin, and Howard cut themselves off from civilization and lose themselves in the Sierra Madre. Unable to recognize what the "real treasure" is, Dobbs regresses and (both literally and figuratively) loses his head—like Kurtz in Conrad's *The Heart of Darkness*, he cannot cope with the implications of darkness, and he finds only death. Though likewise motivated by gold, Howard is the one most prepared for the journey—he is the one who makes the crucial decisions, and only he knows how to find and mine the gold—and he has a strong enough sense of self to come through the journey intact. Also, he learns what the real treasure is, a sense of human commitment, as he chooses finally to remain with the Indians as their doctor. Curtin, however, is the one who learns the most. At first similar to Dobbs in his greed, his quick temper, and his tendency toward violence, he displays in addition a moral sense that Dobbs lacks: in refusing to let Dobbs steal Howard's gold, Curtin acts according to conscience and to a social ethic that indicates his own developing commitment to humanity.

Like Chaucer's "The Pardoner's Tale," *Sierra Madre* is an example of the three-companion version of a common folk tale pattern, "the treasure finders who murder one another."[12] In his novel, Traven enhances the archetype with his detailing of the Mexican and Indian culture, treating his reader not only to a dramatic tale of adventure, but also to a richly textured account of a civilization that was dear to him. His style is, at best, awkward, for although Traven was multilingual and managed to write both in German and in English, the language of his adulthood and his more natural mode of expression was German; as Michael Baumann points out, even Traven's English prose has a "Germanic quality."[13] But while the style is thus often cumbersome, Traven yet displays a dramatic flair and an innate story-telling ability which serves him well in his best novels, wherein the adventure-yarn quality, if not the rather heavy-handed symbolism, of his tales contributes a strong measure of narrative and thematic power.

John Huston's film version of the novel is a rousing adventure narrative, beautifully paced and expertly put together. It features excellent acting from the three principals, Walter Huston as Howard, Tim Holt as Curtin, and Humphrey Bogart (cast against type) as Dobbs. James Agee, in his rave review of the film, labeled Huston second only to Chaplin as "the most talented man working in American pictures," and commented that the story "is told truly and beautifully."[14]

Though Agee's evaluation of Huston now seems a little excessive, his praise for the film's construction remains accurate—it does possess that classic Hollywood style, so unselfconscious and fluid that its audience is drawn totally into the illusion of reality. While remaining generally faithful to the novel's central plot, Huston shies away from much of the psychological/archetypal underpinnings of Traven's narrative and also considerably simplifies the characters. He also tones down Traven's cynicism, and even, to a large extent, his pessimism—Huston's film is more open and optimistic than its original, his characters more likable and easier to identify with. Huston has a tendency (evident in *Moby Dick* and *The Maltese Falcon* as well) to ignore the more tragic/absurdist implications of the works he is adapting. Philosophic digressions (such as the story of Flitcraft in *The Maltese Falcon*) are difficult to handle in film, and Huston, who is always more interested in movement than in reflective dialogue, naturally avoids them. His *Sierra Madre*, then, becomes a vigorous tale, full of action and male comraderie; what little of Traven's world view does emerge in the film seems almost accidental, remaining undeveloped and largely circumstantial.

The film, like the novel, opens in Tampico, concentrating on Dobbs. But where Traven's Dobbs is introduced sitting on a bench, merely contemplating his destitute state, Huston's stands in front of a list of lottery numbers, where he learns that his is not a winner and tears up his ticket. The active physicality on this sequence immediately characterizes the film's Dobbs, who is constantly on the move in the opening scenes. When he sees his hope for quick money in the lottery evaporate, he immediately hits the streets to beg, and he succeeds in getting money, not once but three times, from a prosperous-looking American in a white suit (played by John Huston). Unlike the passive and as yet indeterminate character of the novel's opening, the Dobbs of Huston's film is quickly sketched and set in motion—clearly he is an aggressive fellow, and that is a trait an American audience can admire. Huston also introduces the lottery motif early, for it will play an important part later in the film, when another lottery ticket wins money for Dobbs. The second time it seems to Dobbs and to the audience that his luck has changed, though, ironically, the money then enables him to buy the necessary equipment to go prospecting, which is only the beginning of more trouble than he has been in before.

Huston's Tampico bears little resemblance to Traven's outer circle of hell, whose displaced inhabitants are forever outside society. Again, avoiding Traven's metaphoric allusions, Huston pictures just a small, dusty Mexican town—not a particularly forbidding or even unpleasant place, it seems. His camera does not dwell on the setting, but provides only a rough, atmospheric impression of place and populace; this is hardly the modern dung heap Traven describes. The same is true of the Hotel Oso Negro, whose structure and inhabitants were described in great detail in the novel: Huston provides merely a glimpse of the interior, as Dobbs and Curtin pick up blankets at the desk. Then, as they enter the crowded sleeping quarters, the scene mostly enveloped in shadow, they and the viewer are caught up in a tale about gold being told by Howard, who eventually comes to occupy the entire frame. When Howard finishes talking, the men go to bed, and the hotel is never seen again.

The episode of Dobbs' journey with Moulton into the jungle to find work at some oil-camp is also eliminated, as Huston seems in a hurry to get his men off hunting gold as quickly as possible. The film's opening sequences are designed primarily to introduce the three principals and bring them together quickly. After Dobbs has successfully begged some money and had a meal, he walks over to a park bench and there meets Curtin (in the novel, they don't meet until much later); soon afterwards, they meet again on a ferry ride to work on an oil-rigging site for Pat McCormick (Barton MacLane). Again, whereas Traven describes this place as another hell in a land full of them, Huston spends little time on it, quickly bringing Curtin and Dobbs back to town, where they encounter Howard at the hotel.

Howard's voice is heard, telling a group of men about the perils of looking for gold, before he is actually seen. Then, he fills nearly the entire frame, the camera concentrating on him and his words. While Howard speaks, Dobbs and Curtin become part of the group; they are both a little drunk, and while not actively participating in the discussion, they do listen as they prepare for bed. Here an especially well-constructed shot suggests the psychological dimension of the novel: in angled deep-focus, Dobbs appears in the middle, with Curtin in shadow behind him, and Howard on the right side of the frame in front of him. Thus the partnership is thematically defined—Howard, the wise and temperate sage in the foreground, Curtin, who is at this point known only as a soft-spoken and seemingly decent fellow, in the rear, and caught between them, Dobbs, who needs to grow towards becoming either a Curtin or a Howard; he doesn't, of course, and so remains an irrational id figure, uneasily harnessed between the ego (Curtin) and the superego (Howard).

A more Huston-like sequence follows, as Curtin and Dobbs discuss prospecting for gold the next morning. They spot McCormick, who has not paid them for their work on the oil rig, walking along the street with a woman on his arm. When they approach and ask for their pay, McCormick invites them for a drink at a bar, buys them a few drinks, and tries to get out of paying their wages. He starts a fight, but Curtin and Dobbs overpower him, alternately punching him in the face. The fight scene is paced very deliberately and slowly, in contrast to the quick action typical of Hollywood fistfights: when a man hits the floor, he seems to slide slowly—getting up seems an effort, throwing a punch an agony—Huston's camera emphasizes the empty spaces and the difficulty of movement. When McCormick is finally beaten, he crawls toward the camera, which picks him up at a distorted angle; then his helplessness is emphasized when Dobbs kicks him and rolls him over, his face coming to rest directly in front of the camera. Finally, Dobbs counts out the money he and Curtin are owed, throws the rest on McCormick's bloodied face, and leaves. Thus two points have been established simultaneously: Dobbs is seen acting sympathetically and even admirably, as he takes only the money he is entitled to, and he is here strongly linked with Curtin, as the two join together for the violent confrontation which so often in Huston films develops the theme of male comraderie. The parallel scene in the novel is not at all violent, for there, when McCormick sees that he will not be able to overpower the men, he pays them off and leaves. Traven, clearly, is more interested in presenting McCormick as an unscrupulous capitalist; Huston, in the visual-narrative possibilities of the episode.

After getting their money from McCormick, Dobbs

suggests that they go prospecting for gold. Fired with enthusiasm, he feels sure that there is a great deal to be had for a minimum of effort. Curtin is more practical and suggests that they take Howard along. He is delighted to join them. Each puts up his share of the money (Dobbs is able to help Curtin pay his share because of the winning lottery ticket), and the partnership is formed. The final shot of the sequence shows Dobbs and Curtin shaking hands; then the camera closes in to show only their clasped hands, with Howard skeptically looking on in the background—his look suggests that he knows what is going to happen, for he understands the tricks that gold can play with men's personalities.

Huston cuts next to the three men riding on a train, which is soon attacked by bandits. Their leader, El Jefe (Alfonso Bedoya), who wears a gold hat and flashes gold teeth, will become a symbol of the dark power of gold, the very personification of evil. (Here Huston translates one of Traven's inset narratives, Lacaud's tale, into the main plot of the film, involving his three protagonists directly in its expository action.) In quick cuts, Dobbs is shown confronting El Jefe, at one point nearly shooting him. When the bandits are at last driven away, Dobbs laments that he just missed killing the man with the gold hat: his casual regret—"sure wished I got him"—takes on ironic overtones, in light of what happens to him later.

The men arrive at Durango, where they buy burros and supplies and start off on their journey into the wilderness. Dobbs and Curtin quickly learn how difficult prospecting is and how merciless nature can be, Huston emphasizing the men's difficulty as they hack their way through the bush and walk through windstorms and torrential rains. Dobbs and Curtin soon become dispirited and angry, but Howard retains his jauntiness, apparently tireless and confident. In the evening he eats his beans with relish and plays the harmonica, while his partners, too tired even to eat, fall asleep.

Dobbs is already beginning to show signs of wear. Frustrated and unable to accommodate himself to nature or to his partners, he is soon ready to give up; Howard merely laughs at his partners' inexperience:

> What's that you say, go back—well, tell my old grandmother! My, my, my—what great prospectors! Two shoe clerks reading the magazine about prospectin' for gold in the land of the midnight sun, south of the border and west of the Rockies! . . . Let me tell you something, my two fine fellows, you're so dumb, there's nothin' to compare ya with, you're dumber than the dumbest jackasses. You're so dumb ya don't even see the riches you're treadin' on with your own feet!

To Curtin and Dobbs he appears mad, but Howard is right—he points up to a mountain, as the camera follows on a long pan, indicating where the gold is.

In the following scene, Huston focuses directly on the gold: Howard is panning by a stream, when, in extreme close-up, some few unimpressive granules are left in his pan—here, in its natural state, gold looks, disappointingly, like little more than sand. Preceded by the dramatic panning shot up the mountain, which was accompanied by blaring martial music, this visual undercutting by contrast of the precious substance itself neatly deflates the glorious pretensions of the quest. The close-up all but devalues the concept of gold, suggesting that the dream is as insubstantial as sand, and Huston will re-emphasize this later when the gold, indistinguishable from the dust it mixes with, is blown away at the story's end.

Finding and processing the gold works an immediate change in Dobbs—one evening as Howard is weighing up the day's take, Dobbs wants to know "when are we gonna start dividin' it up?" Again Huston composes his shot effectively, with Dobbs lying down in the extreme left of the frame, only part of his face visible, the rest clouded by cigarette smoke, and Howard, sitting up, dominating the frame, as he explains why, because of his age and slowness, he is the most trustworthy of the group, the one who should be allowed to safeguard the treasure. As Stuart Kaminsky points out, when a character in this film lies down, "he generally speaks more honestly than when he is standing"[15]—as if in a confessional, or dream situation, he reveals his innermost thoughts and motives. Dobbs takes offense at Howard's remark that he (Dobbs) might run off with the money, and at the suggestion that the partners will have to hide their shares from each other; Dobbs' own anxieties are coming to the surface, though he hotly denies them. When Howard starts dividing the gold, Dobbs sits up and the camera focuses on his face, his eyes fixed on the scales as he makes sure that he is not deprived of a single grain.

Next, a swift montage sequence indicates the passage of time, and then Dobbs is shown working in a cave. A sudden cave-in is followed by a very quick reverse-angle shot, showing the cave as a dark hole. Dobbs seems literally and figuratively trapped within the womb of the Sierra Madre, the prisoner of his own greed. Seeing his plight, Curtin hesitates briefly—for the first time displaying an ignoble impulse— before rushing in to save Dobbs. Regaining consciousness, Dobbs remarks, "I owe my life to you, partner"—but he will eventually repay the favor by trying to kill Curtin.

Huston carefully differentiates his protagonists in a scene by a fire as they discuss what they plan to do with their money. Howard thinks about setting up a business and enjoying his remaining years in a quiet small town, while Curtin, in one of the film's more lyrical moments, tells of his days as a fruit-picker, emphasizing the comraderie of the group's singing, drinking and working together, and dreams of owning his own orchard. Dobbs has a narrower vision of things: he wants fancy clothes, loose women, and a lavish meal, and concludes with a private fantasy—he would like to go to "a swell cafe . . . order everything on the bill of fare, and if it ain't just right—or maybe even if it is—I'm goin' to ball the waiter out and make him take everything back."—the victim longs to become the victimizer. Here it becomes increasingly clear that Dobbs is the misfit in this questing trio, and Huston multiplies the evidence against him by simplifying Traven's characters and upsetting his careful balancing of personal traits. Whereas Traven arranges that the men save each other's lives various times, in the film, only Dobbs is saved (thereby deepening the impression of his ingratitude); in the novel it is Curtin, not Dobbs, who suggests dividing up the gold; and, in a scene similar to the fireside conversation in the film, it is Traven's Curtin who thinks about "dames," while Howard and Dobbs talk about going into business together. Traven's men seem to represent more or less equal mixtures of good and evil impulses— Huston's, less complex, diverge sharply into clear-cut character types, acting and reacting predictably according to the contrastive psychological patterns established early in the film.

The emphasis on Dobbs' separation is increased when he objects to Howard's suggestion of putting a limit on their earnings. At Curtin's remark, "There's no use making hogs of ourselves," Dobbs becomes violent: "Hog, am I . . . I'd be in my rights if I demanded half again as much as you get. . . . There's no denyin' I put up the lion's share of the cash, is there?" The next morning, suspicious of his partners' intentions, Dobbs refuses to go to town for provisions, and later he even draws his gun on Curtin, who has discovered a gila monster under the very rock where Dobbs has hidden his goods. Dobbs backs down when Curtin dares him to put his hand under the rock, and then Curtin turns over the rock and shoots the monster. Unfortunately, he has also exposed the more dangerous monster in Dobbs himself, who never forgives Curtin for humiliating him.

Going into town in Dobbs' place, Curtin meets a Texan named Cody (Bruce Bennett)—Lacaud in the novel—who questions him about gold. Curtin tries to parry his questions and leaves, but he is followed back to camp. Once again

Dobbs becomes the aggressor against the stranger, ordering him out of the camp, but when Howard invites Cody to eat, Dobbs temporarily backs down again. In the morning, however, when Dobbs sees Cody taking water to make coffee, he once again abuses him. Cody's response, "I thought I was among civilized men who wouldn't begrudge me a little fresh water," inflames Dobbs anew and he punches him, another sign of regression (earlier when Curtin referred to his hoggishness, Dobbs was angry, but controlled himself).

The partners are perplexed about what to do with the newcomer. Cody, who suspects that the men have discovered a gold mine, offers them three choices: they can kill him, run him off, or cut him in, only on the profits to be made after his arrival. Howard is impressed by the honesty and fairness of this proposal and favors the third choice; Dobbs wants him killed, and Curtin here indicates the darker side of his nature by agreeing with Dobbs. They are about to execute Cody when they notice a gang of bandits heading their way—again, El Jefe and his gang confront the men. Now Cody is needed for his gun, and the four men ready themselves for a confrontation; in the ensuing gun battle Cody is killed, and the bandits eventually are driven off when a group of *federales* come to save the day.

Throughout the action of the gold hunt in the Sierra Madre, Huston provides an on-going commentary on his protagonists' personal development, and on the developing character of their partnership, through manipulation of his basic *mise en scène:* grouping the men together in recurring three-shot, he indicates their changing moral positions by carefully varying the pattern of arrangement. In the early sections of the film (during the formation of the partnership and the first, wearying days of the search), Howard's superiority to Dobbs and Curtin is emphasized, as he generally occupies the frame alone when he speaks, either in close-up or close-medium shots which guarantee his words the moral weight they deserve. Dobbs and Curtin are then seen

The Treasure of the Sierra Madre: An intruder (Bruce Bennett, at left) confronts the three prospectors (Tim Holt, Humphrey Bogart, Walter Huston), forcing them to reconsider their plans.

together when Huston cuts away from Howard. Once the gold is found, however, the men are usually grouped in a three-shot. As they are processing their first gold, Howard is placed in the middle—he still occupies the moral center—with the other two disposed on either side. During the scene in the tent, when Howard divides up the take, he is still in the center, and when he tells Dobbs and Curtin why he is the most trustworthy of the three, he occupies the frame alone; he is at the center again when the men discuss putting a limit on the take.

As Dobbs' moral disintegration begins, however, and his ethic begins to dominate the group, Huston signals the shift of power by placing Dobbs in the center of his three-shot, as when he takes the lead in hostile confrontation with the newcomer Cody. Here, too, Dobbs' moral and physical disintegration is suggested, as he generally crouches between Curtin and Howard, his hands dangling animal-like at his sides. This effect is confirmed when Cody's insinuation that Dobbs is not "civilized" is answered with a savage punch—when Curtin and Howard emerge from the tent, then, they move to either side of Dobbs. This pattern fluctuates momentarily when the partners consider what to do with Cody: Howard again moves to the moral center as he opposes killing the man, but Curtin's decision to go along with Dobbs' inclination for murder quickly puts Dobbs back in the middle, and Howard, forced to concur, even briefly leaves the frame, his moral leadership in total eclipse.

When the men see that the bandits have been scattered by the *federales*, they go to check Cody's effects, finding a few hundred pesos, a picture of his wife, and a letter from her. Howard begins to read the letter, but has difficulty and turns it over to Curtin—it reveals that Cody was a devoted husband and father, and, in its emphasis on the values of family and land, echoes Traven's sentiments about where the "real treasure" lies. Here again, Huston has taken the moral of one of Traven's digressions (Howard's tale about the chief and his blind son) and incorporated it as part of his narrative; in so doing he finds it necessary to modify the character of Lacaud/Cody, changing him from the novel's mad, eternal prospector into one of the moral spokesmen of the film, a good man whose life touches at least Howard and Curtin. It is appropriate that Curtin read the letter, as his own memories of an orchard at harvest time are recalled in the wife's words:

> I have never thought any material treasure, no matter how great, is worth the pain of these long separations. . . . The country is especially lovely this year . . . the upper orchard looks aflame, and the lower like after a snowstorm. . . . I do hope you are back for the harvest. . . . it is high time for luck to start smiling upon you, but just in case she doesn't remember we've already found life's real treasure. . . .

Here, for the only time in Huston's series of three-shots, Curtin occupies the center of the frame, as he is entrusted with Cody's legacy—a poignant expression of the values of family, roots, and the growth of nature. (Except for McCormick's whore-companion and Dobbs' dream of the "loose women" to accompany his newfound wealth, women are otherwise absent from the universe of the film—the words of Cody's wife suddenly evoke another world beyond this of the masculine quest for gold.)

These life values are reiterated in the following sequence when the men decide to leave: Howard insists that they ought to take time to break down the mine and put the mountain back in shape (here he regains his place in the center of the shot):

> HOWARD: Make her appear like she was before we came. . . . We've wounded this mountain, it's our duty to close her wounds, it's the least we can do to show our gratitude.
> CURTIN: You talk about that mountain like it was a real woman.
> DOBBS: She's been a lot better to me than any woman I ever knew!

Around the campfire at night after they have left the mountain, Curtin suggests giving a fourth of their shares to Cody's widow. Howard agrees, but Dobbs mocks them: "You guys must have been born in a revival meeting."

That evening the partners' talk is interrupted by four peasants who seek help for an injured boy. Howard agrees to go and try to save him. The scene in which he revives the boy has a mystic, religious quality, created in sharply defined light/dark contrasts that provide an almost chiaroscuro effect. There is religious music in the background, and Howard is initially seen in a long shot trying to revive the boy—the composition has the look of an all-male Pièta. Huston cuts between Howard and the peasants who watch, and then, when the boy revives and Howard rises, the crowd of villagers forms a path for him to make his way back to the camp. It is a moving moment, emphasizing once more the values of community and human commitment.

The next morning the villagers insist that Howard stay with them for a time, so he puts his gold in the charge of Curtin and Dobbs, promising to meet them in Durango in a few days. Alone for the first time and deprived of Howard's leadership, Curtin and Dobbs' relationship, as in the novel, collapses almost immediately. During the scenes in which Dobbs is becoming an increasingly more dangerous threat to his remaining partner, Huston dramatizes his disintegration by showing him repeatedly in the crouching position, at one point wrapping his arms around his legs in a fetus-like pose. His appearance becomes more disheveled than ever, his beard grizzly and his clothes tattered; squatting by the fire, his face takes on a menacing, satanic look in the flickering light.

Curtin is able to disarm Dobbs on his first attempt to shoot him, but soon Dobbs gets back his gun, pushes Curtin off camera and shoots him twice. After the shooting, plagued by his conscience, Dobbs talks to himself as he sits by the fire, and then Huston concludes the scene rather melodramatically as the flames overwhelm Dobbs and the whole frame.

Next Dobbs is shown crawling along on his stomach and pulling the burros, regressing to a reptilian stage. He notices a water hole and thrusts his head in to drink. In the water appears a reflection of El Jefe, disheveled like himself—Dobbs and his evil alter-ego are thus joined in the dual image. Shortly thereafter El Jefe kills Dobbs with a swing of his machete, presumably decapitating him as in the novel, though Huston restricts his effect to a shot of El Jefe lifting the machete and the sound of the blow as it strikes Dobbs.

The bandits search the burros and find the sacks of gold, which they split open and empty, scattering the gold dust to the wind. Later, in the village, when the mules are recognized as those sold to the Americans, the bandits are captured and executed. The execution scene concludes with a shot of El Jefe's gold hat blown over the graves by the wind, a reminder of the link between Dobbs and the bandit leader, both of whom have lost their heads to the impulses of greed.

Howard and Curtin, who has been saved by some Indians and treated by Howard, ride into town and learn of Dobbs' death. After talking with a boy who overheard the bandits speaking about some sacks left at a mission, they ride through a windstorm to the mission, only to discover the empty, ripped sacks being carried about by the wind. When Howard regains his composure, he begins to laugh hysterically, echoing the speech of his counterpart in the novel, and Curtin soon joins in.

Sitting against a wall, the two men then discuss the future. Howard decides to stay with the Indian peasants and serve as their medicine man. At first, unsure of what he will do, Curtin accepts Howard's offer of his share of what the burros and hides will bring if he will visit Cody's widow during harvest time. Unlike Dobbs, who, unable to assimilate the darker side of himself, met it head on and died, Curtin and Howard will re-enter human society, Howard to become a healer, and Curtin, perhaps, to marry Cody's widow. Curtin, clearly, has absorbed much of Howard's wisdom—as they mount up and depart, Huston's camera lingers on Curtin after Howard has left the frame, stressing the centrality of his growth progress in the tale. The film's final image, however, is of a cactus and a torn gold sack, a last allusion to Dobbs, who chased after an empty dream and found only the wasteland in his own soul.

Huston remains basically faithful to Traven's novel, adapting many plot sequences and much dialogue directly from the book. His most significant alterations involve the tale's ending and the nature of the characters themselves. While Howard is clearly the most positive character in the novel, he is not there so thoroughly "good" as Huston presents him, while Curtin, throughout most of the novel, is no better than Dobbs, joining, for example, in his open hostility to Lacaud (Cody), and himself originally suggesting the divisive policy of nightly distributing the gold. The assignment of less complex roles to the protagonists perhaps reduces the psychological dimensions of the story, but, for the purposes of film, Huston's simplifications work well. He improves on Traven's narrative line, pacing the adventure/quest plot masterfully—action is the natural language of the screen, and Huston knows how to employ it, developing his characters through their actions, not through their thoughts. Most of *Sierra Madre* is shot in middle distance, providing ample space in which the characters can act and react, as well as supplying a convenient frame within which to explore the relationships of the characters to each other and to their surroundings. Even Huston's sophisticated constructions have a natural look—only after repeated viewings do their symbolic significances become openly apparent.

Sierra Madre is thematically similar to much of Huston's other important work. He is characteristically concerned with the concept and nature of the quest, and his best films reflect this archetypal interest: in addition to *Sierra Madre* and *Moby Dick*, such films as *The Maltese Falcon, The Asphalt Jungle, Beat the Devil,* and *The Man Who Would Be King* exploit this motif. The quest is always important, and often dangerous, and the object of the quest (usually wealth) is generally attained, but Huston is primarily interested in its effects on the individuals involved (the group is usually small and male-dominated). He ascribes great importance to the search itself, the value lying not so much in attaining the goal as in the striving for it, and Huston obviously admires the hardy, robust quality (underlined in his visual style) of his adventurers—even Dobbs is a figure of some stature in his determined pursuit of his private dream.

Huston's admiration and his fondness for the quest, however, is tempered by his distrust of wealth. Traven ends his novel with Howard riding off with the Indians; Huston concludes his film with a shot of the cactus and the tattered, rag-like sack. *The Man Who Would Be King*, which very much resembles *Sierra Madre*, ends on a similar note—a close-up of Daniel Dravot's (a Dobbs-like character who becomes corrupted by power and wealth) decayed head topped with a shining gold crown. Poignant symbols of human folly, either image might serve to illustrate Sam Spade's ironic concluding line in *The Maltese Falcon:* "The stuff that dreams are made of."

6

MURDER IN
THE FIRST DEGREE

THE NOVEL
Paths of Glory
(1935, Humphrey Cobb)

THE FILM
Paths of Glory
(1957, Stanley Kubrick)

Stanley Kubrick, who directed the film of *Paths of Glory*, is one of the most respected of contemporary directors, and he is certainly deserving of the praise showered on him by critics and film scholars. However, the record of commentary on this film points up a central weakness in the "auteur" theory that credits him with primary responsibility for the film's content[1]: in discussions of what is generally referred to as "Kubrick's *Paths of Glory*," no mention is made of Humphrey Cobb's novel, from which is derived much of the film's power, as well as its basic story.[2] While Kubrick and writers Calder Willingham and Jim Thompson have changed the focus and toned down some of his narrative's brutality, Cobb yet remains the ultimate source of the film's drama and of most of its ideas.

In April of 1934 Cobb, deciding that he was tired of his desk job at an advertising agency, sat down to write a novel; in August he completed *Paths of Glory*. Upon its publication, various critics predicted wide sales, and the Book-of-the-Month Club adopted it as its main selection for June of 1935. The book seemed to have the makings of a best-seller, but after selling well for a few weeks, it quietly disappeared. Cobb never published another novel—perhaps he felt he didn't need to, for all of his feelings about war are explicitly represented in this one short, powerful, and highly emotional work. Cobb (who died in 1944 at the age of 45) would probably have been pleased that his one novel was translated to film by so great a director as Kubrick, who, while changing some of the narrative emphases, yet managed to create from it one of the most memorable anti-war films ever made.

Humphrey Cobb was the son of distinguished parents: his father, Arthur M. Cobb, an artist, and his mother, Alice Littell Cobb, a physician, were both Bostonians, who were, at the time of their son's birth (on September 5, 1899, in Siena) living in Florence, Italy, in a house once owned by Robert and Elizabeth Barrett Browning. The Cobbs remained in Florence until Humphrey was thirteen, in the meantime sending him to school in England. In 1913 the family returned to America, where Humphrey attended school three years before being expelled for insubordination. In September, 1916, he went to Montreal, enlisted in the Canadian forces and sailed from Halifax the following April. Because of his youth, he was held in England for a year, but then was sent to the front, where he saw a great deal of action with the Royal Montreal Regiment of the First Canadian Division. Twice he was gassed slightly and, according to his own account, "mildly annoyed because he was hit by various pieces of flying metal but never properly wounded."[3]

The war that Cobb fought was a totally horrific experience for which none of the participants—statesmen, generals, or soldiers—were prepared: the European leaders who had driven their countries into conflict had not foreseen either the extent or the duration of the blood bath that would follow. It was a war that no one really knew how to fight: professional soldiers were unprepared for technological warfare; generals, unable to cope with the vastly increased firepower of machine war, failed to stock enough ammunition to carry out their initiatives. Stanley Cooperman explains, "Only in World War II did the machine achieve mobility; in 1914 officers thought in terms of infantry, of cavalry, of 'flanking,' of 'advance,' of 'engagement.'"[4] As a result of such ineptness of command, many of the major battles resulted in staggering numbers of casualties for no tangible accomplishment—the battle of Verdun saw the killing of a million men and yet the position of the front line did not change.

The generals did not seem to be aware, either, of the tactical application of the weapons at their disposal. Céline wrote, in *Journey to the End of Night,* "Everyone queued up to go and get killed," and Cooperman draws the inference: "It was a war of determined but absurd blood letting, a senseless reiteration of futility and callousness."[5] It was a war of attrition, a degrading, filthy experience, reducing men to the level of "human cattle." There could be no dignity even in death, for, as Cooperman points out, under the conditions of modern warfare,

> . . . "fighting" became a passive rather than an active procedure; the vast majority of casualties on both sides was incurred among soldiers who at the moment of their deaths were either groveling on the earth, fighting desperately among themselves for shelter, or playing interminable games of cards in trenches or rear-echelon posts. The man was separated from the act; the potential hero could be—and often was—splattered by a stray shell under circumstances that had nothing whatever to do with soldiering.[6]

Paths of Glory is a grimly realistic account of the physical wretchedness of trench warfare—the mud, the inability to move, the stench of the battlefield—all is revealed with an eye for detail that few war novels can match. Cobb also captures the crippling, paralyzing effects of fear and emotional exhaustion. Ultimately, however, the sheer brutality of the spectacle is subordinated to his main theme, the exposure of the absurd and tragic gap between the officers and the enlisted men. Few American war novels have so damned the military power structure.

His narrative's vivid evocation of the ugliness of warfare and of the psychology of the soldier no doubt reflects Cobb's own war experience, but the plot of the novel is based on a true incident reported of the French army. Cobb's fictional re-creation was inspired by an article in *The New York Times* in 1934, headlined "French Acquit Five Shot for Mutiny in 1915; Widows of Two Win Awards of Seven Cents Each," and by an account in a French journal by a widow who had managed to clear her husband's name and had been awarded token damages by the French government.[7]

Some details of the actual story are changed for the novel: the real Company Five becomes the 181st Regiment, the evil of command is personalized in the figure of General Assolant, and the story involves the execution of three men rather than five. The novel consists of three chapters, which determine its structure: the first introduces the principal characters, the regiment, and the larger arena of the war; the second describes the futile attack on "the Pimple," a German-held position which the French command feels it must capture; the third describes the procedures of the court martial, for cowardice, and subsequent execution of the three soldiers.

Briefly the novel focuses on the 181st Regiment, which has been withdrawn from the trenches for a much-needed rest. A communiqué arrives at command headquarters, mistakenly announcing the capture of the seemingly impregnable German position known as "the Pimple." Because the army commander wishes to avoid the embarrassing situation of correcting an official communiqué, he orders General

Assolant, division commander of the sector, to take the hill within forty-eight hours. The 181st is called back from its prospective leave and ordered to attack. Meeting with heavy German fire, the soldiers find it impossible to advance, and most of them are killed, some even before they can leave the trenches. Outraged over the failure of the attack and primarily concerned for his own reputation, the general accuses his men of cowardice, thereby setting them up as scapegoats for the incompetence and the inhumanity of himself and his superiors in the hierarchy of command. After some cold-blooded calculation of appropriate numbers of sacrifices and some accommodation of political and personal influences, three soldiers are eventually executed and proclaimed "examples" to the remaining survivors of the attack.

In an appreciation of *Paths of Glory*, Warren Eyster tells of his asking William Faulkner if he had read the novel: "He answered rather testily that Humphrey Cobb was a hack journalist, hardly worth serious discussion."[8] The book was, however, in Faulkner's library, and he did admire it enough to borrow from it incidents and characters for his novel, *A Fable* (1954),[9] which is also set in World War I and deals with the failure of a French regiment to attack an impregnable German position. Faulkner's peevish dismissal, a characteristic evasion through half-truths, probably stemmed from a feeling that the novel was not literary enough, in the sense that it lacked the aesthetic depths of psychological complexity, symbolic structure, tonal variation. Eyster, too, takes the novel to task for lacking the scope of Tolstoy's *War and Peace*, the thematic and formal resonances of Crane's *The Red Badge of Courage*, and the archetypal significance of Hemingway's war novels.

This is not entirely correct, for there is some symbolic structure in Cobb's novel, and, although the narrative is, for the most part, quite direct, it certainly transcends mere reportage. Indeed, it has the ability, as L. H. Titerton observed, to sweep "the reader off his feet by the sheer force of its truthfulness."[10] Cobb's description of the attack on the Pimple is an illustration of this power:

> Whistles sounded along the jumping-off line.
> Charpentier climbed onto the smoking parapet, shouting and waving to his men to follow. He stood there, waving and shouting, an heroic-looking figure, fit for any recruiting poster. He did not feel heroic, though. All he felt was the blister on his heel and the intoxication of the vibration all about him.
> Men started to scramble over the parapet, slipping, clawing, panting. Charpentier turned to lead the way. The next instant his decapitated body fell into his own trench.
> Four other bodies followed right after his, knocking over some of the men who were trying to get out. Three times the men of Number 2 Company attempted to advance, and each time the parapet was swept clean by the deadly machine-gun fire. It couldn't be done, that was all. The men, with one accord, decided to wait.[11]

Cobb's vision is one of total despair; the greatest enemy of man is man, and there is nothing redeeming in nature. Unlike Hemingway's heroes, who can find solace within themselves or in some code of dignity and professionalism, Cobb's characters find only silence or further confrontation with the absurdity that war represents. His tragic perspective is clearly displayed early in the novel: Lieut. Paolacci, temporarily in command of Number 2 Company, is leading his troops on a patrol when they are surprised by explosives dropping around them, and Cobb invests the scene with dramatic, Poe-esque imagery, reminiscent especially of "The Pit and the Pendulum" in terms both of description and of theme. The dominant landmark which the company is patrolling is a chalk pit, "a circular excavation situated in the southeast right angle formed by the intersection of the road and the narrow-gauge track" (p. 37). When the explosives start, Paolacci is hit, and Cobb's description is graphic and obviously allusive: "It tore through his pelvis, carried his whole right hip away, and knocked him over the edge into the chalk pit. He tumbled down, down, down . . ." (p. 40)—the effect recalls that in the "Descent into the Maelstrom," as Poe's narrator falls "down, down, down" into darkness, into the realms of chaos and the absurd where one becomes overwhelmed by visions of despair. The narrator of "The Pit and the Pendulum," significantly, is more terrified of the pit than of any of the tortures his captors have prepared for him, for he instinctively knows that it hides the greatest terrors, the darkest knowledge. When Paolacci wakens, he finds himself in the pit; the moon reveals rats (another Poe echo), and the "smell of horse dung" fills his nostrils. Panicking, he screams out: "For the love of Christ! Help help! I'm dying. I'm all alone. . . . Here, in the chalk pit! Jesus!" (p. 45), but "his shrieks echoed back and forth on the walls of the chalk pit." Man is alone, and his prayers for help are unheeded.

Like Poe's narrator, Paolacci wants to measure the outlines of his world (the rational mind persists in believing in reason), but he, too, only discovers further horrors. In one of the most moving and terrifying scenes in the novel, Cobb's descriptive facility combines with a distinctly macabre sensibility to suggest the grotesque situation of man and the absurdity of his fate:

> Paolacci began to feel the pain in his shoulder. He also felt a lump between his shoulder blades. He realized he wanted to get up and climb out of the pit, then waited for the desire to become more impelling. While waiting, his right hand began to move in exploration. It came in contact with the obstruction wedged against his cheek. His [sic] pushed and it gave way, the smell of horse dung receding with it. He moved his head gingerly to look at the thing. It was his own boot, unmistakably. How did it get there, near his face? He formulated the will to straighten his leg out, but there was no response. His hand moved downwards, feeling over his own body. . . . He groped for his thigh and couldn't find it. Instead, his hand entered an enormous, sticky cavity which seemed lined with sharp points. . . .

Gradually with weary patience and persistence which was constantly being thwarted by waves of silent delirium, he untangled the chaos of his life. He had been hit by that shell. . . . In falling into the chalk pit, his leg had been buckled back diagonally under him, and he was now lying on it, with his left cheek against his own heel.

. . . Fever was rising in him, giving comfort to his body and ineffable peace to his mind. The terror of being alone and helpless had gone. He closed his eyes the better to appreciate the delights of his hallucinations. . . .

Later still, when the shadow cast by the moon was rising again on the side of the chalk pit, a rat climbed noiselessly up the jamb of the gallery entrance and watched Paolacci for a while. Then it stepped forward daintily, jumped onto the lieutenant's chest and squatted there. It looked to the right and to the left, two or three times, quickly, then lowered his head and began to eat Paolacci's under lip. (pp. 46–47)

Paolacci has explored hell and discovered the inadequacy of his own body; the world is revealed as a mud hole infested with rats; death, not dignity, God or nature, is man's only refuge. (This passage nearly anticipates the "Snowden's secret" episode of Joseph Heller's *Catch 22*, although in Cobb's universe there is no Yossarian to benefit from the "secret," but only the rats, and the surrounding darkness.)

Nature, here, is indifferent, seeming to mock man's misery. The central action of the novel takes place in the spring, which indeed becomes the "cruelest" season, holding back its gifts and appearing even to conspire to make things worse: the continual rains only create mud, which impedes movement and frustrates activity. Instead, it is man's death which contributes to the flowering of spring: "Langlois saw that it was really spring. He saw the delicate blades of grass which the bodies of his comrades had fertilized" (p. 65). Langlois, a man of poetic temperament, sees nothing comforting in nature:

He saw the smoke-puffs of shrapnel being blown about by light breezes. He saw birds making love in the wire that a short while before had been ringing with flying metal. He heard the pleasant sound of larks up there, near the zenith of the trajectories. He smiled a little. There was something profoundly saddening about it. It all seemed so fragile and so absurd. (pp. 65–66)

This natural beauty is counterpointed with the horror that man has created, the grisly spectacle of destruction. A soldier, entering his first battle, is surrounded by its sights and sounds, as Cobb's very cinematic novel offers the equivalent of a subjective shot:

The star shells were becoming fewer, but the light remained nonetheless. The bombardment was now drumfire, and the air was heavy with the smell of explosives. It was getting harder to see the flashes of the detonations because the darkness of the night was thinning. But the earth continued to jump and rock, and whole sections of trench caved in, crumbled and lay still, smoking a little. The wire zinged to the flying metal and chunks of it, thrown aloft by the shells, came down and fell into the trench. (p. 64)

Because death is so omnipresent, there is no real state of innocence in Cobb's world. Trapped in the absurdity of trench warfare, man cannot hope for survival; Eyster writes, "Death was a lottery with a daytime and nighttime quota of six to the hour, with a higher risk rate, of course, during the sunrise bombardments."[12] In an exchange with a fellow soldier before the attack on the Pimple, Langlois claims that he would rather be gunned down than bayonetted, which, he says, "proves that most of us are more afraid of getting hurt than of getting killed" (p. 94). This man's contemplation of death, especially his comment that he would like to die because "it's the only absolute thing in life. It has a mystery and perfection all its own," becomes very ironic, for he will be selected for execution, a victim of the military structure's arrogant refusal to deal with a simple bureaucratic error. Langlois will discover that his death has no mystery, and that his life is regarded as meaningless.

If trench warfare and the absurd conditions of the universe are subjects for Cobb's despair, man's contempt for his fellow man, embodied in the inhumanity of the military power structure, is the focus of his anger. The book burns with rage, the intensity of his indignation proving at once the novel's central weakness and the source of its great power.

The army's general staff is here accused and convicted of a total disregard for human life: the soldier is simply a pawn in the staff's war games, which are played to win promotions and decorations. General Assolant, the man ordered to see that the Pimple is taken, reflects this callous attitude when plotting the attack with Col. Dax, who is in charge of the 181st regiment:

> . . . Say, five per cent killed by their own barrage (a very generous allowance, that). Ten per cent lost in crossing no-man's-land, and twenty per cent more in getting through the wire. That left sixty-five per cent, and the worst part of the job over, the most exposed part. (p. 82)

The men are, in his mind, mere statistics: waste and destruction are so commonplace that death is hardly noticed. Indeed, the condition of the men almost bears him out: they are walking automatons, emotionally and physically drained. Langlois describes them early in the novel:

> . . . look at their faces. See that sort of greyish tint to their skin? That's not from sitting in a café on a Sunday afternoon.
> . . . Take a look at their eyes. They're open, but they have the look of not seeing much of anything. They've had it tough, all right. Their eyes are glazed. They're nearly all of them constipated. . . . (p. 8)

Assolant is obsessed with the idea of taking the Pimple and winning his star. During the battle he becomes so enraged at the troops' failure to advance that he orders one of his divisions to fire on his own men, but the battery commander refuses. The attack, impossible to begin with, is over in half an hour; the regiment has been decimated, but the battle positions remain unchanged.

Still indignant, Assolant places the surviving remainder of the regiment under arrest, directing them to await punishment at the Chateau de l'Aigle. The site chosen is significant of his punitive intention, already settled:

> It was the place where the President of the Republic, no less, would pin the star of a Grand Officer of the Legion of Honour on General of Division Assolant's right breast. What more fitting then, than that those who had cost him his star should pay the debt on the same ground. The woods would make a good backstop for the execution posts and there was plenty of room for the regiment to form in three-sided square so that no one would miss the spectacle. (p. 111)

His utter disregard for the lives of his soldiers is again made apparent when he starts dickering about how many men should be shot as examples: declaring at first that he will execute one entire section from each company, he is bargained down, by a more rational superior, to twelve, and ultimately settles for one man from each of the four companies. When Col. Dax objects to the procedure and suggests that he only be shot as an example, General de Guerville replies, "I think you're overwrought. It isn't a question of officers." (p. 117)

The process of choosing the scapegoats is equally arbitrary and equally obscene. Selection is left to the company commanders, each of whom reacts differently to the responsibility. Didier, a brave soldier, is picked by his commander, Lt. Roget, because he has witnessed Roget's cowardice during a night patrol, which directly resulted in the death of the third member of that patrol; Didier's death will effectively silence him and keep Roget's reputation secure, at least for the moment. Sancy, another company commander, chooses his victim in a scientifically detached way, actually enjoying dealing with the problem, and the prospect of playing God. When his aide, Arnaud, criticizes him for the injustice of his approach, Sancy replies,

> "Who said anything about justice? There's no such thing. But injustice is as much a part of life as the weather. And you're getting away from the point again. He isn't being shot for a crime he didn't commit. He's being shot as an example. That's his contribution to the winning of the war. An heroic one, too, if you like." (p. 139)

He narrows his choice down to Férol and Meyer because both are social undesirables, people who will not be "needed" by France after the war; Meyer (child molester, syphilitic, and a Jew) seems more undesirable, but Sancy finally picks Férol (mentally defective and a chronic alcoholic) because he is afraid of being accused of anti-Semitism and possibly involving the army in another Dreyfus affair. Langlois is the third man selected—his company has simply drawn lots, and his is the "winner." Capt. Renouart, the fourth commander, refuses to participate, insisting there were no cowards in his unit, and because his name is the same as that of a high-ranking politician to whom it is feared he might be related; this refusal is allowed, and no fourth victim is designated.

The court martial, too, is a mockery of justice: no indictment is read, no transcript kept. The men are forced to admit that they did not advance, but no extenuating circumstances are permitted mention. The defense attorney is not even allowed to call witnesses to testify as to the men's good character. The formalities are carried out quickly and efficiently, the men summarily convicted of cowardice and sentenced to death by firing squad.

In jail, waiting to die, the men are individualized in their

Paths of Glory: The three scapegoats (Joseph Turkel, Timothy Carey, Ralph Meeker) are executed, pawns in a treacherous game of military justice.

responses to the situation. Férol remains brutishly passive, apparently uncaring, and is only concerned with smoking and drinking. Langlois' letter to his wife is the one tender, and fully human, moment in the novel:

> We love each other and we have constructed, from two lives, one life together, one which is ours, which is wholly of ourselves, which is our most precious possession, a beautiful, satisfying thing, intangible but more real, more necessary than anything else in life. We have applied our effort and intelligence to building, expanding, and keeping the structure in repair. Somebody suddenly steps in, not caring, not even knowing who we are, and in an instant has reduced our utterly private relationship to a horrible ruin, mangled and bleeding and aching with pain. (p. 187)

Obviously, in the universe of *Paths of Glory*, this isolated island of two is the only prospect for human happiness, and it is a tragically vulnerable one. Didier, too, writes to his wife, describing Roget's cowardice and explaining that he has been framed. His anger and frustration erupt in violence when a priest comes to offer the men last rites. Langlois refuses, preferring to "live through this night alone," but Didier, enraged at the priest's empty pieties, kicks him in the stomach. Langlois tries to subdue him, and eventually Didier is knocked unconscious by a guard, who also breaks his leg.

This mishap does not, however, delay the execution. Langlois, before being led out, observes that "fear and pain are the complete neutralizers of sexuality"; earlier he has noted that battle conditions similarly affect the bowels— "when men get scared they get tense and things inside them solidify. Functions stop." (p. 8) Caught up in the inhuman circumstances of war, man clearly ceases to be human, and it does not matter that Didier's injury now renders him insensible, for he has become no more than a beast for the sacrifice, conveniently objectified and at the disposal of his "superiors." Cobb's naturalistic imagery enforces the point:

after the execution, Didier's lifeless body is described as looking "like a pack animal that had collapsed and perished under the weight of its burden."

The execution scene is a model of realistic-emotional description, peculiarly cinematic in its attention to detail and in Cobb's technique of cutting between drum rolls, the tying of the prisoners to the posts, the feelings and looks of the prisoners. The situation is directly symbolic: "Of the three, Didier more nearly maintained the illusion that a crucifixion was in progress"; Langlois remarks, "Those posts make it look like the Crucifixion, don't they? And if we keep in this order, it will be Férol who will play the role of Christ" (p. 203). (Faulkner would be heavily influenced by this scene when he described the death of the corporal in *A Fable*.) At last Langlois himself assumes the significant posture in the moving passage of description that follows the fatal volley:

> One bullet had struck Langlois in the leg and he began to sag in that direction. His ropes had not been cleanly cut by the volley which had ripped through his intestines and lungs and he was left dangling there, his arms caught to the post. He wavered a little, grotesque and pitiable, as if pleading to be released, then slipped a little farther down so that he seemed to be abjectly embracing and imploring his post. (p. 207)

At this point the novel concludes abruptly upon the delivery of the *coup de grâce*.

Cobb would publish a serialized novella, *None But the Brave*, in *Collier's* in 1938, which contains a number of stirring battle scenes and descriptions of men under fire. Undercut, however, by some formula plot devices involving a *ménage à trois* and the friendship of two men, it lacks the power of contained emotion that distinguishes *Paths of Glory*. In Cobb's obituary *The New York Times* reported that he left an unpublished manuscript entitled "November 11, 1918: The Story of the Armistice"; in addition, he spent some time in Hollywood and shares screen credit (with Peter Milne) on the film *San Quentin* (Warner's, 1937), which starred Humphrey Bogart, Pat O'Brien and Ann Sheridan. At the time of his death, he was working for an advertising firm in New York City.

His lone novel has remained influential, providing material that other writers could use and shape for their own purposes—reflections of its narrative situation may be seen not only in *A Fable*, but also in Herman Wouk's *The Caine Mutiny* and Norman Mailer's *The Naked and the Dead*, which also deals with a futile assault on a mountain. *Paths of Glory* itself, finally, was dramatized for the stage by Sidney Howard and filmed by Stanley Kubrick. Cobb's was a small legacy, but a powerful and affecting one.

Two major changes, one a structural re-emphasis in the highlighting of a single protagonist, and the other a revised perspective on the story's ending, constitute the principal influence of Kubrick and his writers in transferring Cobb's novel to the screen. Col. Dax, a distinctly peripheral figure in the novel, becomes the film's central character (played by Kirk Douglas), and his personality is modified to suit the larger function. In the novel he is not portrayed as the brave, idealistic man he becomes in the film; in fact, Cobb first describes him as nearly overwhelmed with the dread of battle:

> Neither Vignon nor anybody else suspected for a moment that Dax, colonel of the 181st Regiment of the line, of the crack Assolant Division, next on the list for a general's stars and a promotion in the Legion of Honour, four times cited for bravery in Army Orders—no one suspected for a moment, so well did Dax conceal the fact, that he was in a state of fear which was rapidly turning into panic. (pp. 29–30)

This fearful tendency never surfaces in the film, where Dax alone seems entirely fearless. In the film, he also assumes the function of the prisoners' attorney—at one point he is described as "one of the leading lawyers in France." By means of such dramatic condensation, Kubrick thus switches the central emphasis from the men (Cobb's focus) to Dax, who serves as a convenient mediator between the two opposed worlds of the film, the world of command and the world of the soldier.

Kubrick also adds a coda to Cobb's ending: concluding savagely upon the *coup de grâce* after the execution, the novel leaves the reader emotionally drained, angry and shocked by the senseless killing, but Kubrick chooses to carry on the story beyond this point. In the film, General Mireau (Assolant in the novel; played by George Macready) is informed by General Broulard (Adolphe Menjou) that there will be an inquiry into his order to fire on his own troops. When Mireau leaves, the audience knows that he has been disgraced and that he will certainly resign and perhaps even kill himself; some retribution is offered as a consolation for the murder of the men just witnessed. This is followed by a scene in a tavern where the soldiers are introduced to a frightened German girl (played by Susanne Christian, Mrs. Stanley Kubrick), a refugee, and the only German character to appear in the film. The men at first behave like animals, hooting and whistling, but when the girl begins to sing a song (about a mother hearing of the death of her son in war) the men quiet down and then join in, some beginning to weep. Kubrick thus softens the novel's harsh conclusion by closing with a scene which emphasizes the common humanity of all these victims of the brutalities of modern warfare.

Kubrick structures his film in the contrast between two settings; that of the grand chateau where the commanding officers live and devise their vicious strategies amid the splendor contrived by the equally tyrannical and unfeeling aristocracy of another era, and that of the trenches, confined and filthy, where the soldiers live and wait to die. The film opens, ironically, with the *Marseillaise*, played ominously as the credits appear against a black background; then a title appears on the screen: "France, 1916." Next a narrator sets the scene for the audience (a favorite device of Kubrick's, this opening narration recurs in *The Killing* [1956], *Spartacus* [1960], *Dr. Strangelove* [1964], *A Clockwork Orange* [1971], and *Barry Lyndon* [1975]), telling of Germany's attack on France and of France's brave countermeasures, which have succeeded in reversing earlier losses: by 1916, "after two years of grisly trench warfare, the battle lines have changed very little. Successful attacks were measured in hundreds of yards and paid for by hundreds of thousands of lives."

The narration is spoken over a shot of the chateau, as a squad of soldiers form two neat columns in front of the door. The emphasis on military symmetry and precision, strict in its inhuman formalities, quickly becomes a visual metaphor for the world of the chateau; as he will later do in *Barry Lyndon*, Kubrick focuses his camera insistently on the stiff, almost statuesque compositions emblematic of a world which can transform men into columns, supportive, in the architectural sense, of the "glory" and the grandeur of these new despots of the post-revolutionary society. This suggestion of a new feudalism, embodied in the army hierarchy and mirrored in the incongrous elegance of the chateau, is subtly confirmed when Gen. Broulard enters the room: as he strides through the door in an assured, military manner, he seems utterly at home in this environment, and he adopts its privileges easily, handing his coat and hat to a soldier/servant behind him without a glance, secure in the knowledge that some underling (walking coat rack) will be there to attend to his needs.

After some greetings and a smug reference to the luxury of his surroundings, Broulard tells Mireau that he wants him to take the Anthill (the Pimple of the novel). At first Mireau refuses, saying that his men are exhausted, but Broulard flatters him and whets his ambition with the possibility of a promotion. (Here, taking the Anthill is a direct order, not the result of a bureaucratic mishap, as in the novel.) This sequence is interestingly shot: as Broulard speaks, he leads

Mireau around the spacious room in a choreographed, winding pattern, suggesting how Mireau is being led morally astray (he requires little prompting). Kubrick's camera follows them in increasingly widening circuits which emphasize the dizzying grandeur of the setting (an echo of German expressionism?—the film was shot in Germany) as Mireau moves further and further away from reason.

Kubrick then cuts from the chateau to the trenches, introduced by a binocular view of the Anthill (this shot will be repeated four times in the film to emphasize the distance of the command from the actual fields of battle). The trenches, naturally, comprise a direct antithesis to the elegant chateau world; their shape, narrow and rudely linear, confines the camera to a graceless tracking movement as it explores the chute-like path. The contrasting patterns of movement appropriate to the two major settings here points to another strain of visual imagery by which Kubrick underlines the unequal nature of the military society: restricted to simple, relatively safe lateral moves within the trench itself or the tentative, and usually fatal, forward plunges necessary for attack, the infantry soldiers are the pawns in a great, destructive chess game; conveniently characterless and featureless (the word "pawn" is, in fact, derived from a medieval Latin term for "foot soldier"), they are considered readily expendable in the service of the ornately variegated figures, more powerful in their complex movements, who line up behind them, directing the combat in their own interest. Of a strictly quantitative importance in the game, the soldier/pawns exist only to be sacrificed, their neat columns of formation providing at the beginning a solid front which is to be disordered and decimated in the maneuvering for tactical victory.

Abruptly transported from the chateau's baroque spaciousness to this cramped and constrained trough of the pawns, Mireau is next seen touring the trench in an apparent attempt to bolster his troops' morale. Self-conscious and clearly out of place, he greets individual soldiers with unvarying condescension: "Hello, soldier, ready to kill more Germans?" Two of the men he speaks to, Férol (Timothy Carey) and Paris (Ralph Meeker), will later be executed at Mireau's orders, while the third, Arnaud (Joseph Turkel), is in the frame during a third confrontation: thus Kubrick deftly introduces the victims (although his audience, on a first viewing of the film, is ironically no more likely than Mireau himself to recognize the individuality of these men).

Mireau then enters the dugout of Col. Dax, whose "residence" echoes the confinement of the trenches. Kubrick frames the scene to emphasize Dax's integration with his surroundings: despite his status as an officer, he obviously belongs in the world of the soldier. Mireau, on the other hand, is uncomfortable in Dax's dugout, continually crouching, his elegant uniform endangered by falling debris. In addition, he is forced to speak to Dax from behind, because of the lack of space, and several medium and close shots in the sequence re-emphasize the confinement of Dax's headquarters as opposed to the expansive elegance of Mireau's. Here, too, Kubrick introduces another visual device that will recur throughout the film: many of the scenes of significant personal confrontation are shot in dark places with single sources of light. Dax's dugout is lit only by an overhead lamp, beneath which Mireau is placed at times, causing the light to shine directly on his face with an eerie, and accusatory, effect (the light in these scenes is always directed upon the evil character, never on a protagonist).

During this scene, Mireau pressures Dax to agree to lead the assault on the Anthill by threatening to relieve him of his command if he refuses. Dax's ennobling idealism is displayed twice, once when he objects to a remark made by the general's aide (Richard Anderson) who compares the men to cattle, and again when he resists Mireau's chauvinistic urging by scornfully quoting Dr. Johnson's remark that "patriotism is the last refuge of a scoundrel." Also during this meeting, Mireau echoes Assolant's speech in the novel about the percentage of casualties to be expected, and again the callousness of command is stressed. (Kubrick's critics often praise this dialogue as one of the most effective scenes in the film, again failing to notice that it is taken directly from Cobb's book.)

Kubrick eliminates most of Cobb's battle sequences and reconnaissance missions, focusing instead almost exclusively on the gap between officer and soldier. He does, however, retain the night patrol episode involving Lt. Roget (Wayne Morris), Paris (Didier in the novel), and Lejeune (Ken Dibbs). The film's plot here follows the novel closely: Paris has no respect for Roget, his former classmate, whom he knows to be a coward and a drunk, but Roget is an officer and so Paris must obey his orders. On the evening before the battle, they go out to scout no-man's-land; Roget is shown drinking heavily before the expedition. The sequence in no-man's-land is composed dramatically: the men crawl through the mud and wire at night, the camera occasionally shooting them from above to emphasize their smallness and the limitations of the body. Roget breaks up the patrol by sending Lejeune ahead, and soon a flare lights up the sky, giving the scene a nightmarish, carnival-like quality. When Lejeune does not return immediately, Roget panics, hurling a grenade into the darkness and running back to the French lines. Paris, however, proceeds forward and finds Lejeune's body in a hole, disfigured by the grenade. Next, Paris confronts Roget in his dugout, in a scene that parallels the earlier meeting between Dax and Mireau. Here, Paris accuses Roget of cowardice and murder, while Roget makes it plain that it would be difficult for an enlisted man to bring charges against an officer. Again, the exchange is shot in gloom, with a single light which shines, this time, on Roget.

The battle scene (the only one in the film) is justly famous. Just before it, the camera tracks behind Dax as he reviews the troops, at times even shooting subjectively, standing in for Dax (unlike Mireau, who strode along in the camera's direct view, himself the object of attention, Dax actually notices the men themselves, his and the camera's focus taking in their faces and their situation). The lighting is gray, and parts of the sequence are shot through smoke, from which the soldiers seem to loom grotesquely. The attack begins with Dax climbing a ladder and blowing his whistle to lead the charge. Kubrick shows the men pouring onto the field of battle, again making them seem ant-like in a high, overhead shot. Then he shifts to a side view of the troops sweeping across the open space, achieving an extraordinary double perspective in conveying at once a sense of documentary-like realism and a horror-inducing, expressionistic flavor. Long shots primarily capture the realistic effect, while some of the close-up shots have an orchestrated, ballet-like quality. In this sequence, too, Kubrick employs a handheld zoom lens, honing in on Dax, presenting much of the scene from his point of view as he watches his men being butchered and his ranks thinning out.

The sounds of the battle are effectively counterpointed against Dax's whistle, which he blows defiantly but which seems frighteningly weak and futile against the thunderous barrage of gunfire and explosives. The attack on the Anthill, by implication, is as futile as trying to hear a whistle above the din of battle.

Another shot of the battlefield seen through binoculars provides the transition back to command headquarters, where Mireau is raving, calling his men "miserable cowards" because of their inability to advance. He orders an artillery captain to fire on the men, but the order is refused. Mireau then orders the company placed under arrest, as the scéne shifts to the chateau. There, in the company of Broulard and Dax, he demands that the men be executed. (This is the first time Dax has been seen in the chateau, and, seated between Mireau and Broulard, he seems cramped and uncomfortable.) As in the novel, the officers bargain over the number of men to be killed (here Dax vainly defends the men), their purely quantitative interest in death recalling the pre-battle predictions of likely percentages of casualties. Finally it is decided that three men will be shot and that Dax will defend them at the court-martial.

The scene shifts to the prison, where Dax explains the situation to the prisoners; again a single source of light, this time sunlight streaming in through the cell windows, illuminates the sequence. The condemned soldiers differ somewhat from those in the novel: Paris is a combination of Didier (selected because Roget wants him out of the way) and Langlois (he has Langlois' sensitivity and is given some of his lines in the film), and Arnaud, the soldier chosen by lot (Langlois in the novel), also possesses some of Langlois' attributes, for he has been decorated for bravery and is articulate about his plight. Férol is based on the character of the same name in the novel (chosen because he is deemed a social undesirable, though here he is obviously not a serious deviant), but he lacks that original's nihilistic and animalistic ways. In the novel, Férol is exclusively concerned with liquor and cigarettes, and he goes uncaring to his death, for never respecting life, he has no fear of death; in the film, he seems simple and a little slow, but he is enough afraid of dying to confess to the priest, and he walks to his execution clutching a rosary and sobbing uncontrollably. Kubrick thus induces immediate sympathy for all three victims because, not having concentrated on their characters earlier in the film, he must now force the audience to adopt them quickly as protagonists.

The court-martial is filmed skillfully so as to emphasize the inhumanity and the ritualistic, game-like quality of the proceedings: the prisoners are marched into a room at the chateau and seated at attention, each with guards in rigid attitudes on either side. The floor, with its black and white tiles in a chessboard pattern, provides a graphic reference to the power game to be played out here, and when the prisoners are called, singly, to approach the judges and speak, the camera shoots from in front of them, isolating the ineffectual, pawn-like movements, forward and back, to which they are restricted here as well as on the battlefield. The judges appear in shadow in front of the prisoners, while the camera also takes in the attentive guards behind them: the shot emphasizes their entrapment, for they seem caught between the judges and the guards, and entirely defenseless in their immobility. The officer who serves as prosecuting attorney, in contrast, is shown in front of the judges, whose backs are now in shadow, and, in a manner reminiscent of the sinuous progress of Broulard and Mireau as they strolled about, conspiring together, in the film's opening scene, this man, the deputy of their arrogant and selfish authority, is now seen winding easily around the table, supremely confident that he will win the case. Dax, on the other hand, is shot from a low angle, his exaggerated physical stature reflecting his moral superiority; his concluding argument is viewed from behind him as he walks between the prisoners and the bench, attempting vainly to connect the two worlds between which he is the only mediator.

Prior to the execution, Kubrick adds an incident, not found in the novel, which briefly raises some expectation that the men may yet be saved: the officers are holding a dress ball at the chateau, the dancers whirling about in elaborate circles, again reiterating the visual motif of the opening scene. Dax enters and tries to persuade Broulard to stop the execution; when he refuses, claiming that the example will be good for the troops' morale, Dax informs him that he has depositions to prove that Mireau ordered the artillery commander to fire on his own soldiers. A close-up of the shocked expression on Broulard's face as he considers the implications of this action, and Dax's efforts to hammer home the potential embarrassment to the command creates some momentary doubt as to the fate of the scapegoat soldiers. Kubrick, however, then cuts, ironically, to the execution scene, which becomes all the more devastating in the shock of this last-minute failure to place the blame on the true "villain" of the piece. Despite his defensive maneuver, Dax has failed, and so the pawns must be sacrificed to the military hierarchy's need to cover the tracks of its own tactical incompetence.

The execution scene displays the same dramatic geometric patterning which has earlier emphasized the men's powerless status in the dual game of war and military politics; in addition, an incessant drumbeat supplies a measured echo of the ceremonial significance of their doom. Throughout the execution sequence, the chateau looms in the background, its grandeur menacing and yet mocking the spectacle taking place in front of it. Between the stiff ranks of troops assembled to witness the execution, Paris marches to his death with military dignity, while Férol, sobbing and clutching at the priest, and Arnaud, unconscious on a stretcher, seem all too human in their lack of military discipline. The camera then tracks relentlessly toward the three stakes; the men are tied, blessed by the priest, and shot.

As mentioned earlier, Kubrick spares his audience the pain of ending on such a note, first, by introducing an element of partial justice (at this point in his career, he lacks Cobb's all-consuming pessimism) and, lastly, by picturing the soldiers in a moment of emotional unity. After the execution, Mireau is called before Broulard and disgraced for his vengeful attempt to fire on the men. (There is an echo of an earlier scene in which Dax has punished the selfish malice of Lt. Roget by placing him in charge of the firing squad, thus forcing him to take immediate, physical responsibility for the killing of Paris, whom he framed; in that scene, again, the light in Dax's dugout was focused accusingly on the face of the culprit.) Finally, while the soldiers are seen in the tavern, whistling and frightening the girl, Kubrick cuts to Dax's face (he is listening outside the door), which registers disgust at this further spectacle of human cruelty. But then, the men calm down and the girl's song moves them to tears, as they sing with her; again Kubrick cuts to Dax, whose face now reflects some acceptance, some recognition that there is something humane and noble in man, something worth saving. The film concludes upon Dax's being informed that the men have been ordered back to the front.

Paths of Glory is a virtually flawless film—every frame is effective, every sequence necessary. Also, it is marvellously acted, as Kirk Douglas gives one of the finest performances of his career (he would give another for Kubrick in 1960 in *Spartacus*), and the supporting cast is excellent, especially Adolphe Menjou (who manages to steal the film with his suave and sinister complacency). Kubrick's dramatic exploitation of setting, visual imagery, lighting, and music, finally, give the film an exciting emotional and symbolic intensity that highlight the story's grotesque significance.

Despite his modification of Cobb's ending, Kubrick yet preserves and projects Cobb's thematic focus on the impassable gap between officer and soldier, and the abject vulnerability of the soldier's lot. *Paths of Glory* is, indeed, a clear example of how a great film artist can form and shape his literary original even while delicately transforming it for his own purposes. In his next military film, Kubrick's personal vision would come even closer to Cobb's: in *Dr. Strangelove*, no one is spared as he concludes his damning study of the military structure with a nuclear holocaust, in which everyone and everything is finally destroyed.

7

THE GANGSTER
AS EXISTENTIAL HERO

THE NOVEL
Low Company
(1937, Daniel Fuchs)

THE FILM
The Gangster
(1947, Gordon Wiles)

The Gangster was released ten years after *Low Company*, the Daniel Fuchs novel on which it was based. Neither novel nor film was a commercial success, and both remain relatively unknown today—though, unlike the other paired works discussed here, this film is probably less well known than Daniel Fuchs' novel. Even studies of the gangster film ignore it, despite its complex relation to the genre. In addition to its generic interest, however, the film invites attention as a rare example of an author's adaptation of his own significant work of fiction for the screen. The final screenplay of *The Gangster* is Fuchs' work—although certain compromises were made along the way (a common enough practice with Hollywood films), no other writer tampered with the script. Fuchs himself altered his novel significantly for the purposes of film, recognizing, as few other literary artists have been able to do, the special properties and problems of the film medium and the need for creative reworking of the fictional material in its transition to the screen.

Fuchs has worked successfully in both media, and his route to Hollywood was typical of the experience of many writers of his generation. He was born in 1909 on Manhattan's Lower East Side, the son of immigrants, who settled eventually in Williamsburg, just across the bridge in Brooklyn. This place, an even poorer section than the Lower East Side, would later dominate Fuchs' literary imagination and shape his world view. After high school, he attended New York's City College, where he majored in philosophy and graduated in 1930.

Fuchs came to artistic maturity during the Depression, but unlike many of his contemporaries, his work was not shaped by it. Produced during the decade that brought the radical novel to the forefront of American letters, Fuchs' work remains conservative and essentially apolitical. In fact, in his first two novels, he gently mocks the notion that political solutions can cure the ills of mankind. It was probably because of this unfashionable political neutrality that his works were scantily reviewed and consequently neglected by readers and scholars alike.

Fuchs wrote three novels during the thirties, and they appeared in quick succession. *Summer in Williamsburg* (1934) is the story of a young writer's struggle to forge an artistic vision from the chaotic experience of life in the ghetto. In trying to fathom the reasons for the suicide of a neighbor, this protagonist is told that in order to understand, he must "make a laboratory out of Williamsburg," and so Fuchs' first novel becomes a panoramic reconstruction of Williamsburg life. Here, enclosed in sweltering tenement cubicles, are poor Jews hungering for a piece of the American dream—caught between the high principles of their religion and the realities of tenement life, they flounder in a limbo world of fading dreams and bitter truths.

Homage to Blenholt (1936), not as ambitious a project as *Summer*, is tighter in construction and more surely controlled than its predecessor; it is also lighter in tone, comic rather than descriptive, and not so full of the oppressive summer air that permeated that first study of Williamsburg. *Homage* fully explores the chasm between aspiration and reality: its hero, another young man of Williamsburg, dreams of glory and success, and the novel develops ironically around his plans to attend the funeral of Blenholt, the commissioner of sewers, whom he reveres as someone who surmounted the mediocrity and flatness of his age. The funeral, the novel's centerpiece, and a highlight of Fuchs' fiction, turns into a shambles, as Blenholt is revealed to have been a cheap thug, a mob politician, and a diabetic whose sweet tooth caused his death. From such disasters Fuchs' protagonist eventually learns the lesson of life, that he must face reality and abandon his foolish dreams—Fuchs can love the dreamers, but he knows this world is no place for them.

Both of these novels were favorably reviewed, *Homage* even prompting the *New York Times* critic to proclaim, "The date of Daniel Fuchs' next novel should appear in red on the calendar."[1] However, discouraged by the poor sales of these and his third novel, *Low Company* (1937), Fuchs for a long time abandoned the form altogether, turning a fourth novel into stories which he could sell for good prices to magazines such as *Colliers*, *The New Yorker*, and *The Saturday Evening Post*. In 1937 he was offered a thirteen-week contract by RKO—he accepted and went to Hollywood, where, like many Eastern writers, he became dissatisfied and turned out some anti-Hollywood pieces, including "A Hollywood Diary" (*New Yorker*, 1938) and "Dream City or the Drugged Lake" (*Cinema Arts*, 1937). However, offered another contract in 1940, he decided to return, and this time he stayed to become a very successful screenwriter, earning credit for the scripts of such films as *The Big Shot* (1942), *Criss Cross* (1949), *Panic in the Streets* (1950), and *Storm Warning* (1951). In 1955, his original story for the film *Love Me or Leave Me* earned him an Academy Award; his last screen credit was for *Jeanne Eagels* in 1957. Since then, Fuchs has published a fourth novel, *West of the Rockies* (1971), which takes the film industry as its subject, and a collection of stories, *The Apathetic Bookie Joint*, was published in 1979. In 1947 he adapted his masterpiece, *Low Company*, for release by Allied Artists as *The Gangster*.

Low Company is unlike Fuchs' earlier novels in theme and technique. The heroes of those first two novels were young dreamer-seekers, bent on exploring their universe and discovering their places in it. The serious and sad tone of these books was interspersed with comedy, as Fuchs maintained a kind of Chekhovian balance in his material—though ultimately he, too, had to tip the balance toward the tragic. In *Low Company* this quest-like vision has disappeared, as Fuchs is no longer searching for solutions. Irving Howe has written:

> In his first two novels he had tried to develop themes and construct images that might carry his work beyond himself and to the shores of some general meaning; but in his last novel he acknowledged skillfully and sadly, that his quest for meaning was at an end. He had searched but had not found. . . .[2]

What was to be his last novel for thirty-four years is almost devoid of comedy, exposing a clear perception of the degeneration of man and a consequent sense of despair. In exploring the society that the Depression has shaped, he provides a gallery of characters all locked within themselves, trapped by their inadequacies and temperaments and victimized by a society that encourages their dreams but delivers nothing. Anticipating Nathanael West's *The Day of the Locust* [1939], Fuchs provides a crowd of silhouetted figures—the cheated, the wounded, the nameless many—as a background against which the actions of the main characters take on their full significance. These foreground figures, then, are the fully embodied portraits of modern disintegration.

Low Company presents a wasteland vision, a portrait of a world on the verge of collapse, though its dominant tone is one of compassion. The novel can, in fact, be read as a prose "Waste Land." Not a literal transcription of the poem, it does, however, portray essentially the same kind of world that Eliot depicted. *Low Company*, too, is preoccupied with ugliness, decay, violence, and the disappearance of the human—in the novel Eliot's "unreal city" becomes Neptune Beach (Fuchs' version of Brighton Beach), which is described as a place without foundation or substance: "The sidewalks were broken in all those places where the blocks caved in. . . . Everything in Neptune Beach was sand. It was misery. . . . Nothing was solid, neither the pavements nor the foundations of the buildings."[3] Most of the action takes place at Ann's, an over-decorated ice cream parlor, featuring loud colors and futuristic designs. Here one may lose oneself in unreality; the squalor of the city can be left behind, and the routine, commonplace nature of life (Fuchs calls it "the flat-dishwater of reality") can be swallowed up and replaced by promises of "amour and glamour."

The protagonists are all indigenous to the Neptune Beach milieu, and the action of the novel takes place within about forty-eight hours during which their lives become intertwined and their destinies are worked out. The human element is ultimately the force that shapes Neptune Beach and makes it what it is. The novel opens with an epigraph from a prayer said on Yom Kippur, the Jewish Day of Atonement. It sums up the reasons for Fuchs' despair, and it reveals the sins of society: "We have trespassed, we have been faithless, we have robbed, . . . we have done violence, we have forged lies, we have counselled evil. . . . O, Lord our God, forgive us for the sin we have committed in hardening of

The Gangster: Shubunka (Barry Sullivan) escapes the city and the
pressure of the organized mob with his girlfriend, Nancy Starr (Belita).

the heart." The key phrase here is "hardening of the heart," for this is the primary cause of most of the sins enumerated in the opening of the prayer. Indeed, it is the basis of Fuchs' greatest despair, for man knows what is good but finds it easier to do evil. Every man lives for himself, no one has time to think of his neighbor, there is no room for kindness or consideration. Man has lost that unique capacity to be "human." In the modern world, Neptune Beach, all have become "low company."

Catering to the needs of these people are men like Spitzbergen, the owner of Ann's. Like most of the characters in *Low Company,* Spitzbergen is driven by a single obsession—his is making money—which makes him a grotesque. (Fuchs displays a rare talenting for thus bending his characters slightly out of proportion, while still maintaining their humanity and reality.) Spitzbergen is, in fact, a successful businessman, but he receives no pleasure from his relative wealth. He "dies a thousand deaths" everytime he has to pay a bill. During the course of the novel he is preoccupied with the weather, as rain is keeping the crowds away from the beach, and his soda fountain is losing business. (Ironically, in Fuchs' wasteland it is always raining, whereas the hoped-for rain in Eliot's poem does not come until the end.) Spitzbergen also owns a considerable amount of real estate, some of which he rents to Shubunka, who uses it for houses of prostitution. Much of the action of the novel concerns the attempt of an organized mob to take over the houses of prostitution run by such small-time operators; they try to push out Shubunka, but he refuses to give up the business that he has spent years building up. The mobsters try to get to Shubunka by pressuring Spitzbergen, which compounds his worries over the inclement weather and the business he is losing.

Shubunka, too, is a grotesque—in his case it is more a matter of his physical appearance than of a mere personality trait. This man's ugliness actually separates him from others, who generally find him repulsive and frightening. He does have a certain sensitivity and displays at times a genuine affection for people (he is the only major character who seems capable of a generous gesture), but he is usually rebuffed. Fundamentally he is a lonely man who yearns for companionship, though unfortunately his repellent looks, fat shape, and "waddling" gait make him awkward, and his attempts at communication generally fail, for people do not respond naturally to his overtures. This pitiable state is balanced, however, by an almost narcissistic obsession with his own ugliness, which prompts him in moments of rejection to seek out mirrors, "to catch a glimpse of his face when it showed sorrow," and which tends to relieve the pathos of his situation and check the sympathy that the portrayal of his unhappiness often creates. Despite his appearance he is tolerated at Ann's because of his money, as he is aware:

> He knew that every time he walked into Ann's they all looked away from him, they wouldn't come near him because he was funny looking, and they hated him, because they saw his clothes and the money he had. . . .But in spite of them he had built up an organization that made money for him almost automatically. Let them all rot in hell. He had the money and they would come to him whether they wanted to or not. (p. 63)

But while he succeeds in business by catering to the loneliness of others, he is unable to help himself. When he is threatened by the mob, he resists and is determined to fight to maintain his position. In one sequence some thugs attempt to change his mind by mercilessly beating him up on the beach. In one of the novel's most poignant and ironic moments, he cries out at his tormentors:

> What am I? A dog? You have no right to do this! It is not the way for one human being to treat another! . . . . . . We must not be like animals to each other! We are human beings all together in this world. Please! I beg you. (p. 151)

The plea for humane treatment is touching, even as it is ironic—it is Fuchs' ultimate comment on the human condition that this demand for decency should come from a man who is struggling to defend small-time prostitution against organized crime. Abandoned and alone, Shubunka eventually decides to give up. He realizes that he can't beat the organization and leaves Neptune Beach, a defeated, lonely figure.

The story of Shubunka and his destruction by the mob is paralleled by a number of thematically related stories; two of the employees at Ann's figure prominently in the action as well. Shorty, the soda jerker, is a marvelous portrait of the pseudo tough-guy. He is a fake, his whole personality a sham—he is the real "hollow man" of the novel, for he has lost claim to his own identity and in its place has manufactured a web of substitute roles which seem to him superior to what he really is. In this sense he becomes an embodiment of his society's great spiritual poverty. Subscribing wholly to the values of the popular culture, he has destroyed his inner self to imitate the tough-guy type perpetuated by the movies. The influence of film on the lives of characters is a pervasive motif in Fuchs' fiction—it provides a main outlet for escape in Fuchs' universe. The movies are also a major cultural force, one which retards and stifles the spiritual growth of the individual. Finally, the movies are a potent cultivator of images—in Shorty's case the ideal implanted is that of the tough-guy, and Shorty has swallowed the image whole.

Shorty is, of course, anything but a tough guy. He is short, bald, and hardly brave, yet he spends most of his time trying to be what he is not, specifically a ladies' man. During the course of the novel he tries to get a date with Madame Pavlovna, the proprietor of a nearby corset shop. She, too, has been influenced by movie images of romance and sophistication—she tends to overly romanticize her past and her late husband, implying that they were once part of European high society—but her affected airs, dress, and speech appear foolish in the world of Neptune Beach. Fuchs further undercuts these absurd poseurs by presenting the illiterate notes they send to each other during the courting process. In these letters, Madame Pavlovna continually puts Shorty off, then finally agrees one evening to go out with him. Shorty is, true to form, only interested in sex, though he, too, claims to be sophisticated and interested in a "relationship."

After treating her to his idea of a high-class date—a movie and then dinner at a Chinese restaurant—Shorty secures an invitation up to the corsetière's apartment, and he thinks he has it made. He tries to manage the situation in her apartment as if he were playing a movie scene of seduction, but, lacking the illusory grace of the screen idol, he cannot achieve the conventional conquest, and his attempts at romance prove disastrous. Madame Pavlovna is not interested in sex but in some vaguely platonic relationship, and her refusal to submit to Shorty's advances at last end the scene in a surreal, Kafkaesque tableau:

> She raised herself from the sofa with extraordinary strength, exploding into a burst of cries and curses. As she rose, she lifted Shorty outspread in the air . . . Beside his short form she seemed a giantess. Shorty couldn't catch his breath. She had him fixed fast with the fringes of his hair in one hand while she slapped his face with strength, each blow stinging until the tears came to his eyes. She went on whacking him, tripping and falling over him, dragging him to the door as she belabored him. Here she almost picked him up bodily and threw him into the narrow hall. . . .
>
> The corsetiere towered over him, her chest heaving. She drew her negligee carefully over her and looked down at him with enormous contempt.
>
> "Cockroach," she said, and slammed the door. (p. 251)

Disgraced, Shorty eventually is forced to face his own inadequacies and accept his humanity.

Arthur, who also works behind the counter at Ann's, is child-like and innocent. He admires Shorty's tough-guy act because he is not perceptive enough to see through it. His innocence makes him very vulnerable, and as a result, the lessons he must learn by the end of the novel take on violent and horrifying implications. Arthur's closest literary ancester is Wing Biddlebaum of Sherwood Anderson's *Winesburg, Ohio* (1919). Like Wing (Fuchs makes the connection in his suggestive description of Arthur's hands) and the other residents of Winesburg, Arthur is isolated and unable to communicate his loneliness. He lives in a world of his own and aspires to be "free as a bird with nothing on my mind, with enough money in my pocket to get along on and a little something extra besides." The achievement of this state is, of course, impossible in Fuchs' universe, but the yearning links Arthur closely with the lost tribe of Winesburg, Ohio, of whom Randall Reid declares, "They are alien from their surroundings, yearning for a lost past or a promised future which will end their exile and fulfill their dreams."[4] This is the promise that Elizabeth Willard dreams about for her son, that Nathanael West's grotesques come to California to find, that Fuchs' people seek in Neptune Beach, and that Arthur finds in the movies. Like West's Homer Simpson in *The Day of the Locust,* Arthur is a representative and embodiment of the vast crowds of empty people who flock to California and to Neptune Beach, people who lead empty lives and yearn for excitement. Arthur *is* the nameless crowd of the cheated, "primitives who have suddenly inherited decadence."[5]

Arthur must face this darker side of himself when Moe Karty, a former accountant ruined by the Depression, who now gambles only on the horses, persuades him, despite his fear and apprehension, to steal money from Spitzbergen's cash register and join him at the track. There he recognizes the desperation of the crowd, and Fuchs describes his reactions in a passage which directly anticipates *The Day of the Locust:*

> To Arthur, sitting high in the stands, the crowd seemed to become a single unit, in constant motion but according to a

definite pattern and design, like the ocean swell and fall, and this was because the people streamed to their destinations in the same channels: rushing to the gambling ring and rushing away from it . . . Everyone smoked cigars and everyone spat. . . . (pp. 164–65)

When Karty loses all the money, Arthur becomes desperate and hysterical (he had meant to return it). Karty assures him that he will get the money back, and Arthur helplessly trails along as he follows Spitzbergen back home on the subway. When Spitzbergen gets off the train, Karty follows him into a men's room and asks him for money. When Spitzbergen resists, they fight, and Karty accidentally kills him:

. . . Spitzbergen squirmed and made retching noises. His hands were feebling scratching at Karty's face, and soon they fell to his shoulders which he began patting slowly and listlessly as a man would in talking to an old friend. Then the squirming stopped, the choking noises stopped and the hands fell down to his sides, softly slapping the wall with the swing. (p. 289)

The violence and the events of the day have overwhelmed Arthur—he learns that he cannot cope with experience:

What a sap he had been, feeling jealous of Karty and Shorty and Shubunka. They could have all the tough talk and ways. Arthur didn't want them. So he was a kid, so he didn't know nothing, so it was better. You had nothing on your mind and that was something money couldn't buy. (p. 283)

With the death of Spitzbergen, the arrests of Karty and Arthur, and the departure of Shubunka, the sun once again shines on Neptune Beach. In Fuchs' wasteland, the death of Spitzbergen (representative of the money ethic) revives the land, though Neptune Beach only revives to the renewed business of the other shopkeepers. Ironically, too, despite the departure of Shubunka, prostitution remains a lucrative business—perhaps even a growing one, now that a bigger, more efficient organization has taken over.

Despite the cynicism of this vision of human society, Fuchs, unlike many of his contemporaries, was not angry. Rather, *Low Company*, like his other novels, is dominated by a sense of acceptance of things as they are, and the tone is one of compassion. Herbert Lurie, another shopkeeper on Neptune Beach, who observes and comments on the people (and who serves almost as Fuchs' mouthpiece in the novel) reflects near the end of the book:

> . . . Lurie knew now that it had been insensible and inhuman for him, too, simply to hate Neptune and seek escape from it. This also was hard and ignorant, lacking human compassion. He had known the people at Ann's in their lowness and had been repelled by them, but now it seemed to him that he understood how their evil appeared in their impoverished lives and, further, how miserable their own evil rendered them. It was not enough to call them low and pass on. (p. 311)

In adapting his own novel for the screen Fuchs took what might be considered liberties with the text. Gone is the novel's rich texture, the various threads of action which determine its theme, plot and scope. Instead the action becomes very compressed and simplified, and the focus is narrowed to one character, Shubunka. Much of the original cast remains, but they have become cyphers in the transition—it is as if Fuchs knew what changes had to be made in the novel, but was too close to the material to make all the necessary sacrifices by eliminating some of the characters entirely. The new title was not Fuchs' idea—in fact, he did not care for it at all—but by drawing attention to the genre to which the film belongs, it does succeed in alerting the sensitive viewer to the variations it plays on a popular American film subject.

The classic gangster film, as it emerged in the thirties in *Little Caesar* (1931) and *The Public Enemy* (1931), chronicled the rise of a poor individual to a position of eminence in the world of crime and ended with his fall and death. Robert Warshow, in a seminal essay on the subject, called the gangster film a tragedy, for the protagonist is doomed to die "because he is under the obligation to succeed, not because the means he employs are unlawful. In the deeper layers of modern consciousness all means are lawful, every attempt to succeed is an act of aggression, leaving one alone and guilty and defenseless among enemies: one is punished for success."[6]

The Gangster is not a success story. Shubunka, here become the single protagonist, is not on the rise, but occupies the same position throughout the film. He is successful, but his success does not match that of Caesar Enrico Bandello *(Little Caesar)* or Tommy Powers *(The Public Enemy)*. He rules no empire, but just a few houses of prostitution. Most important, Shubunka does not crave success, but is happy with what he has. When he is approached by some of the syndicate's thugs who are willing to come over to him for three thousand dollars and offer to make him "the biggest man in the city," Shubunka turns them down: "I'm satisfied the way I am. . . . I don't want to be the biggest man in the city."

Shubunka is not really an ambitious man. He wants to make enough money to be respected but he does not aspire to be "Number One." His tragedy lies not in his success but in his awareness of the essential human condition of being alone. The classic gangster is alone, but his isolation is a result of his success. Warshow writes, "The gangster's whole life is an effort to assert himself as an individual, to draw himself out of the crowd, and he always dies because he is an individual."[7] Shubunka, too, dies, shot down in the street, but unlike the typical gangster-hero, he dies willingly because he has come to an existential awareness of human isolation. At the end he asks to die, because such an end represents for him an affirmation of life's absurdity. His death affirms not the "failure of success" but Fuchs' notion of the death of all values in the modern world. In its suggestion of evil and decay, and even in the squalid character of its locale, *The Gangster* is closer to the *film noir* than to the gangster film, and it is very much a film of the forties.

The other central characters from the novel are retained in the film, but their importance is considerably diminished in comparison to Shubunka. His is the film's story, and the film's meaning is closely related to his character. An opening voice-over narration by Shubunka himself at once establishes him as the protagonist:

". . . I worked the rackets, dirty rackets, ugly rackets. I was no hypocrite. I knew everything I did was low and rotten. I knew what people thought of me. What difference did it make, what did I care? I got scared, sure. You get hurt a little when you fight your way out of the gutter."

Not only does the film, unlike the book, center on Shubunka, but the character itself has changed substantially. Physically Barry Sullivan, who plays Shubunka in the film, does not at all resemble Fuchs' fictional creation.[8] In the novel he is described as an extremely ugly man: "His was a huge face, his jaws like slabs of meat, black with his beard no matter how often he shaved. His thick black hair, combed straight to the side and back, was heavily greased with Polymol . . . his big face, lumpy nose and gross lips . . . rendered him completely ugly, his face on his short thick neck then looking unnatural, like nothing human." Sullivan, while no matinee idol, hardly resembles this description, and nothing (except a scar on his cheek) has been done to make him ugly.

In the novel Shubunka's grotesque appearance is one of the reasons for his isolation, but it also serves as a physical metaphor for the more widespread moral grotesquerie that prevails in this world. However, metaphor and symbolism, as George Bluestone[9] and others have pointed out, do not work well in films. And certainly Fuchs was wise in eliminating them from the screenplay and in transforming Shubunka into a more strictly realistic figure. Focusing almost entirely on Shubunka, the film had to involve the audience sympathetically in his predicament in order to hold interest. Shubunka had to be made into an at least partially admirable figure, and so the character portrayed by Sullivan is scarcely recognizable as the repulsive petty racketeer of the novel. In *The Gangster*, Shubunka's tragedy is also society's tragedy; as the victim of a sick society, he represents every man who gets crushed by the system.

The audience's identification with Shubunka is increased by other changes in his character. The novel's weak and pitiful creature becomes in the film a strong and confident man. In one scene common to both versions, this transformation is most apparent. In *Low Company*, Shubunka and Lurie are walking on the beach when two thugs confront them, telling Shubunka to get out of Neptune Beach. Here he becomes hysterical, crying and then begging the thugs for mercy. One of them, disgusted by Shubunka's appearance, beats him up and leaves him crying and grovelling in the sand. A similar scene occurs in the film, but this time Shubunka is in command of the situation. When approached by the thugs he is not intimidated, but cool, strong, and assured. When one of them (Elisha Cook Jr.) threatens him, Shubunka slaps him around (a reversal of the novel's action). The thugs' threats mean nothing to him and he assures them that he will not give up his operation.

The most significant change from fiction to film, however, is in the addition of Shubunka's girlfriend, Nancy Starr (Belita). Nancy, who plays a significant part in the film, is not in the book at all, which is in keeping with the Hollywood convention of increasing the love interst when adapting books for the movies.[10] In this case, Fuchs has not merely "increased" the love interest, he has invented one. That the film's Shubunka actually has a girlfriend sharply differentiates him from the lonely, grotesque figure of the novel; Nancy's presence accentuates Shubunka's positive qualities and increases the audience's sympathy.

Nancy Starr is a nightclub singer and aspiring actress for whom Shubunka pays rent and provides a maid and showers of gifts. Nancy in many ways resembles the femme fatale of the *film noir*, sexually enslaving Shubunka with her sexy-blonde looks. Colin McArthur, in his study of the gangster film, writes that this "Circe figure" often "entices the hero with her song."[11] In *The Gangster* there is a scene in a hotel nightclub where Nancy is shown singing, the camera focusing on her slow, seductive movements and providing many close-ups of her face. Despite the fact that the scene takes place in a club, only she and Shubunka are seen; he is unable to take his eyes off her throughout the number, in which she promises that "if you will hold my hand . . . I'll take you to paradise." This is highly ironic, since she will eventually betray Shubunka and indirectly cause his death.

Nancy is interesting not only because of her *noir* associations but because Shubunka authentically loves her, and this love is one of the reasons for his fall. In the novel Shubunka is presented as a man who is capable of generous and tender gestures, but their appeal is diminished by the selfish satisfaction he takes in them. In the film he hides his tender feelings, trying not to let them be seen by anyone (this tension is not handled especially well by Sullivan). He seems emotionally stunted because he feels that everyone is low and rotten and not to be trusted. Loving Nancy would mean displaying weakness, letting down the tough exterior he has tried hard to develop over the years while fighting his way out of the gutter. He does, however, let his guard down once with her, revealing a very tender side:

> When I was a kid in the tenements I used to go walking by myself for hours. . . . One hot, dead summer day I looked up and on the terrace of the tenth floor . . . I saw a man and a girl

kissing, embracing. . . . It was nothing, a small thing. I don't think I'll ever forget it.

Shubunka's desire for love is intense, almost visible in the frozen features captured in the many close-ups in the film. But he deliberately suppresses his tenderness and so turns away those who might provide that love.

Shubunka's attempts at tenderness extend also to Dorothy (Joan Lorring), the cashier at Ann's. In the novel Shubunka likes Dorothy and offers her money when she becomes engaged to Lurie; in the film he offers it when she decides to leave her job at Ann's to take care of her sick father. In both cases she refuses to accept his money, in *Low Company* because his ugliness repels her, and in *The Gangster* because she fears him. In both novel and film Shubunka feels that money can buy respect and love, but, although the first commodity is easily purchased, he learns finally that love is not for sale. The desire to succeed by making money has obliterated man's better nature—society's demand for toughness has negated man's soul. Tenderness must be sacrificed (and is soon forgotten) in the drive to be tough and successful, even though that makes the ultimate victories hollow. Those who absorb this knowledge can win the fight to survive in the world of the hardened heart, but Shubunka never quite brings himself to this state and so must die.

Other characters in the film face this test as well. Spitzbergen, who is the owner of Ann's in the novel, has been renamed Nick Jamey (Akim Tamiroff) in *The Gangster*. His basic characteristics, obsession with money and continual complaint about the need to spend it, are retained in the film. He is a weak, unattractive character who is quite willing to play along with the mob if only they will leave him alone and not vandalize his shop. He is equally afraid of Shubunka and of the mobsters and is never sure of where to turn. Shubunka is able to pacify him with money, but the mob's potentially destructive power is a never-ending source of worry.

The film dwells more than does the novel on the more tender aspects of this man's nature. Early in the film Shorty says to Dorothy, "You know, you wouldn't think it just from the sight of him, but that guy is actually in love with his wife." Later Jamey makes a revealing comment:

> My wife, she's different. She listens to me, she's on my side. I miss her. . . . Well, everyone, no matter who's got to have at least one person dear and near to him. It's only human nature.

It is a touching moment, for he is talking to Shubunka, who would like to love but cannot allow himself to make such a commitment. In that same scene Jamey tells Shubunka that he understands Shubunka's basically good nature:

> You don't like the dirty work. You've got no taste for it. . . . You go around putting up a tough front. . . . But you don't fool me. I see inside you. You're not a terrible big shot.

To this remark Shubunka retorts angrily that he is not a soda jerker or a small-time thug. His overreaction indicates that he knows Jamey is right, but he must keep up his tough appearance. This inability to really love, shared by all of the main characters, is one of the tragic themes of *The Gangster*. Jamey's obsession with his business will not allow him to spend time with his wife, and Shubunka must not let his heart predominate over his head. In *Homage to Blenholt* Fuchs called it "the hunting dog ethic," by which one must live if he is not to end up with neither success, nor love, nor respect.

This theme is hammered home in the film's treatment of Karty (John Ireland) and Shorty (Harry Morgan) as well. In the novel Moe Karty is sick with gambling fever. His obsession deforms him and makes him a grotesque, a version of Dostoevsky's spiteful and independent Underground Man. Karty literally lives underground, in the basement of Ann's, having abandoned his wife to devote all of his time to the races. In the film Karty's role has been considerably short-ened, and it remains sketchy and undeveloped. This mania is dropped altogether, and, like the other characters, he is made more human. Grotesques are not often interesting on film, for they rarely succeed as characterizations (as the failure of the film *The Day of the Locust* attests). Karty, whose first name has been changed to Frank in the film, has become a sad, lonely man whose plight invites pity. The film emphasizes Karty's poverty, his alienation from his wife, who is continual-ly trying to get him to come home, and his desperate need to repay the debt to his brothers-in-law. He kills Jamey to get this money but then runs away, frightened, to confess.

Shorty's story is made more comic in the film. In *Low Company*, he is presented as a pseudo tough-guy, a man whose personality has been distorted by the very tough-guy gangster movies whose conventions *The Gangster* overturns. His tough talk is softened in the film, replaced by a knowing manner, but it does not entirely disappear. Here Shorty talks mostly to Dorothy, telling her how much of a gentleman he is and how he can get any woman he wants, whereas in the book he says most of this to Arthur, on whom it has a greater effect. In the film Shorty spends most of his time courting Mrs. Ostroleng (the Madame Pavlovna of *Low Company*), a corsetière who affects an aristocratic air. They exchange illiterate letters and flirt with each other at Ann's, and always their appearance undercuts their pose—Shorty is short, bald, and stupid, and Mrs. Ostroleng is neither attractive nor aristocratic.

At the end of the film he finally gets his date with her and is invited into her apartment. There he makes advances but is slapped and told to leave, after which his major concern is that he has spent seven dollars and ninety cents on the date and gotten nothing in return; Mrs. Ostroleng moans about the dress for which she spent twenty-eight dollars. Again money is everyone's dominant concern; Shorty's sexual preoccupa-tions are a distortion of Shubunka and Jamey's inner problems, as the film continues to explore attitudes about love. Shorty leaves Mrs. Ostroleng's apartment and the scene ends with the shadow of a gate imposed on Shorty, which suggests that he is a prisoner of his own false image. As Shorty stands before the gate trying to get over it, the camera pulls back to reveal the back door of Ann's, wherein Jamey lies dead on the floor, a victim of his own obsession with money. The kinship of the money-hungry and the base-hearted is emphasized visually.

The film's final moments are handled very well. Deceived by Nancy, who leads him into the mob's hands because they have promised to put her in a Broadway show, Shubunka is robbed and left alone and broken. Nancy blames Shubunka for this betrayal, saying that he would not let her love him, that he made her hate him. Shubunka leaves in a stupor and tries to hide in the crowd of amusement-seekers on the boardwalk. Afraid of confronting his isolation, he seeks the comfort of contact with others, but it starts to rain and the crowd disperses, leaving him alone again. An effective medium shot focuses on Shubunka standing alone in the rain, and then a series of sound flashbacks remind him of the life he has led.

Next he seeks refuge in the apartment of Dorothy, the cashier. She is another character who has undergone a major transformation between book and film. Portrayed as a demanding bitch in the novel, she becomes in the film sweet and decent, a rare innocent (thus assuming Arthur's role as the figure who learns to recognize evil). In *The Gangster* Shubunka admires her (she has no boyfriend in the film), but she learns what kind of business he is in, and her fear of him turns to hate. When finally Shubunka seeks refuge in her apartment, she wants no part of him. She blames him for Jamey's death, saying that Shubunka drove Karty to do it by not giving him any money. Her father shows compassion for Shubunka, but Dorothy checks him, saying, "Let him pay for his sins." Her naïveté angers Shubunka and he replies:

> . . . You're sweet, lovely, and good. You're also very young. Pay for my sins. You know what my sins were? I'll tell you. That I wasn't rotten enough. That I wasn't mean and low and dirty enough. . . . I should have smashed Cornell first. I should have hounded Jamey, kept after him, killed him myself. I should have trusted no one, never had a friend. I should have never loved a woman. That's the way the world is. Wait, find out for yourself. That's the way you have to be, the only way.

Having thus declared his victimization by a world that is worse than he has been, he runs out into the street, hears a car pull up, and asks to die:

> . . . Shoot Cornell! You can have the locations, the rackets, all the profits, all the fun. You can have that ulcer eating in your belly. You can start to learn what it is to hate yourself. You can look in the mirror in the morning and day by day see the ugliness creep into your heart, your face. Take it, Cornell, it's all yours.

As he speaks, the car's light, from off camera, shines in his face. Shubunka is ennobled in his final moment—he seems almost holy; he is surely enlightened. With this final speech he earns the audience's respect, and when he has finished, he is shot down in the street. (In the novel Shubunka does not die. He has been ruined but leaves Neptune Beach having learned nothing, remaining a pathetic figure to the end.)

The film ends with a shot of the crowded boardwalk and a narration that is paraphrased from the novel:

> The new day broke hot and steamy. Soon from all parts of the big city the millions would be jamming into the subways for the trip down to the beaches. . . . The neighbors, the storekeepers of Neptune put their newspapers away and prepared for the Sunday crowds. Everyone said what a shame it was, after so many days of rain, that Jamey the soda man wasn't alive to enjoy the wonderful weather.

With the death of Shubunka and the arrest of Karty, the rain stops. The wasteland is revived by the sun.

The end of the film is again interesting as a variation on the classic gangster film. Shubanka is not finally gunned down or defeated by the law, but by another mob. Unlike Rico or Tommy Powers, he does not really deserve to die; his crimes have certainly not been major ones. His fall is due not to an excess of ambition but to his inability to be rotten and low enough to survive in this world. The film declares not that crime doesn't pay, but that in this world sensitive people cannot survive and, by implication, that crime does pay for those underhanded enough. Modern life has eroded man's spirit and he is left with the world of Neptune Beach.

The film is also free of certain typical iconographic features of the gangster mode: the classic gangster's success is measured by his car and his gun, but Shubunka never carries a gun, nor does he own a car (he takes the subway). Shubunka's attitude toward women and the fact that his fall is in part due to his capacity for love, also differentiate this film from the genre. Certainly Cagney's treatment of women in *The Public Enemy* (or the lack of women in *Little Caesar*) in no way resembles Shubunka's attempt to win Nancy's love in *The Gangster*.

The film's departures from the novel are also significant. The novel, a vision of decay, is a work of greater despair than the film. *Low Company's* characterizations, symbolic structure, and use of detail are dark and ugly, as Fuchs rubs his readers' noses in the dirt of Neptune Beach. Little light breaks through the overcast (like the bad weather) and threatening mood. The film's mood is more balanced. While part of the novel's strength lies in its symbolic structure, the film succeeds in a clear explication of theme and in playing on its audience's sense of the conventions of the gangster film. Its characters have sympathetic sides; they are human enough to be easy to identify with and easy to pity. Their stories are touching in ways that are foreign to the novel. While Fuchs' vision is a bleak one in both cases, Shubunka's death in the film is redemptive, a positive gesture. The novel admits no such escape from its dark vision.

The novel succeeds brilliantly in its aims, but the film is less successful. Part of its weakness is in the acting. Belita's performance as Nancy Starr is wooden, lacking feeling and depth. Barry Sullivan's Shubunka, while at times very effective, is not always successful in revealing the complexities of the character. But the major fault in *The Gangster* lies in its incomplete translation from the novel. Many of the changes made were, as has been indicated, dictated by the demands of the film audience, but it seems, finally, that too much has been tampered with. Some of the minor characters, though well played (especially by Akim Tamiroff and Harry Morgan), are so pared down in the transference from fiction to film that they do not succeed in becoming fully-embodied characterizations. Despite the fact that their symbolic functions are de-emphasized, too many symbolic associations remain and not enough character. In a film that runs less than ninety minutes, too many characters are introduced and they cannot be developed properly. Ultimately too much of the film is determined by the novel's symbolic structure, and it never fully releases itself from the limbo world between fiction and film.

The Gangster, however, remains interesting in its defiance of convention and in its creative use of genre. It is lean and spare in construction and possesses scenes of considerable power. It is obviously Fuchs' work (the screenwriter here is certainly the *auteur*), for thematically it is consistent with his work as a novelist. Both *Low Company* and *The Gangster* deserve to be re-evaluated and studied as works of a significant but neglected artist.

THOSE WHO
WALK IN DARKNESS

THE NOVEL
The Pawnbroker
(1961, Edward Lewis Wallant)

THE FILM
The Pawnbroker
(1965, Sidney Lumet)

In an era whose fashion it is to devaluate mankind and deplore the human condition and to do so within increasingly radical experiments in subverting the conventional forms of art, Edward Lewis Wallant's four novels have won few admirers and only scant critical attention. Old-fashioned, a traditionalist in terms of structure and thematic development in his fiction, he wrote to assert the validity of individual experience and even the possibility of human redemption, and so perhaps it is not surprising that his books have sold poorly. Despite the intensity of his vision and his considerable dramatic skill, his work would be virtually unknown but for the popular success of Sidney Lumet's film version of *The Pawnbroker*, his second novel, which has sold well in paperback since the film's release (a new edition has just been issued by Harcourt Brace Jovanovich). For Wallant, who died in 1962 at the age of 36, was a Romantic, out of his time, who insisted upon the necessity of making the difficult, always painful, and often unsavory commitment to life—a commitment which he saw as the only salvation from the alienation and the horrors of modern experience.

Although his works share some characteristics of such other contemporary Romantic novels as Bellow's *Henderson the Rain King,* Malamud's *The Assistant,* and Salinger's *Franny and Zooey,* Wallant's closest ties, clearly, were to the early, visionary Romantic philosopher-poets of the nineteenth century. In an essay entitled "The Artist's Eyesight" (1963), he expressed his artistic credo in frankly Wordsworthian terms:

> Normally we see others only as they relate to our own immediate needs, and for that, normal vision is often sufficient. Yet there are times when we have a need we cannot recognize, a sudden hunger to know what lies in the hearts of others. It is then that we turn to the artist, because only he can reveal even the little corners of the things beyond bread alone.

In each of his four novels—*The Human Season* (1960) and *The Pawnbroker* (1961) were published during Wallant's lifetime, while *The Tenants of Moonbloom* (1963) and *The Children at the Gate* (1964) were released posthumously—it is the central figure's destiny to learn to recognize within himself this "hunger" and to move toward satisfying it through communion with others. As a character in *The Children at the Gate* observes: "We must all hold hands in the dark." This movement toward communion is at the heart of all Wallant's fiction. Each novel's protagonist makes a solitary journey from some state of spiritual and emotional paralysis, through great suffering, to a final, life-restoring revelation of the power of love to redeem the soul.

Joe Berman, the modern-day Job (JoeB/erman) who struggles toward this redemptive awakening in *The Human Season*, contemplates his new awareness in terms that remain valid for the later protagonists:

> Answers came in little glimmers to your soul, most clearly in childhood, in the sounds of certain voices and faces and things, when you feel the miracle and the wonder; and he knew that the Torahs and prayer shawls and churches and saints were just the art men tried to create to express the other deeper feeling. "It's like the light that don't last long enough to recognize anything. But the light itself, just that you see it . . . that's got to be enough . . ." And then more emphatically, almost desperately, for it was his last hope: "It *is* enough!"

Both the imagery and the ideology of this passage suggest a strong linkage between Wallant's vision and the religious mysticism of Thomas Carlyle's Victorian classic, *Sartor Resartus*. Like Carlyle's protagonist, each of Wallant's central characters undergoes a symbolic conversion to a sense of life's meaning, involving a recognition of divine mystery and, ultimately, some kind of compulsive affirmation of human existence. Indeed, Berman's meditative epiphany reads as a kind of synoptic allusion to central concepts of Carlylean Romanticism: the soul's miraculous vision, clearest in childhood, and the symbolic "Church-clothes" of established religion, which both embody and obscure the redemptive Light of creation. Of Carlyle's philosopher-protagonist it is said, "The whole energy of his existence is directed, through long years, on one task: that of enduring pain, if he cannot cure it. . . . only by victoriously penetrating into Things themselves can he find peace and a stronghold" (*Sartor Resartus*, Book Second, Chapter X). Wallant's hero-sufferers, too, emerge through pain to awareness, their peace-giving vision expressed in new commitments to the mingled joy and pain of human life.

   The Children at the Gate and *The Tenants of Moonbloom* are Wallant's most complex, most controlled, and most successful expressions of this faith in the concept of modern redemption—*Moonbloom* is, in fact, a masterpiece, as yet sadly neglected by the critical establishment—but Sol Nazerman, the Pawnbroker, remains Wallant's most powerful protagonist, his dramatic rebirth from a death-like moral limbo providing a stunning image of modern man's spiritual and emotional crisis. Himself a survivor of the concentration camps, he nevertheless lost there his family, his best friend, and his will to participate further in any experience of feeling. Now wholly estranged from his society, he generally encounters the humanity surrounding him, both in his business and in his private life, with chilling indifference. Cut off from the present by his tormenting memories of the past, this character, both in Wallant's fictional portrayal and in Rod Steiger's brilliant film performance, embodies the traumatic alienation that is the legacy of man's history of atrocity.

The novel covers a period of approximately three weeks, from sometime in August to September 28th, fifteen years after the death of Sol's family. The movement is chronological, except for flashbacks to the past, dominated by the horrors of the concentration camp, which are presented with an emotional intensity that is all the more remarkable in that Wallant himself was not an inmate of the camps. These graphic memories recur to Sol mostly in his sleep—while he usually succeeds in shutting out his past during his waking hours, in the dream state he is forced to acknowledge it, to experience feelings that his rational mind denies. The memory/flashbacks depict the whole painful catalogue of Nazi atrocities: his son David's grotesque death in a cattle car on the way to the camp (crushed with his family in the car, Sol is unable to keep his son from falling into the feces on the floor—it is one of the most horrifying scenes in contemporary literature), the forced prostitution of his wife Ruth to a German soldier, the killing of his daughter Naomi and of his best friend Rubin, his own work in the crematoriums, and the experimental operation he had to undergo.

The novel is at once entirely realistic and deeply symbolic. Its principal setting, a pawnshop in Harlem, is vividly detailed, as is the array of tattered humanity which comes there in search of a little money in exchange for the junk they bring from their desolate lives. The atmosphere of the shop and the Harlem locale are clearly evoked, and Wallant's talent for creating a succession of whole characters in a sequence of brief vignettes is employed here to great advantage. In addition, the pawnshop functions as a versatile image in varying contexts. At one point it is described as a vault-like tomb, wherein the dead Sol must work out his salvation.[1] At another point it becomes a kind of debased church, with Sol a priest administering solace in the form of money to his defeated, suffering parishioners:

> . . . I am like their priest. . . .They get as much from me as they do from their churches. They bring me their troubles in the shapes of old table radios and watches and stolen typewriters and gold-plated crucifixes and half-paid-for cameras. And I, I give them absolution in hard cash.[2]

In this connection, the symbolic function of names becomes important. Like the Roman sun god, Wallant's Sol is a kind of god in his own kingdom, dispensing life in bits of money, evanescent rays of hope, to his people. The name also recalls the Hebrew Saul, the first king of Israel, whose successor David (the name of Sol's dead son) was Israel's greatest king and, according to the New Testament, an ancestor of Christ. Jesus, then, is the name of Sol's assistant in the pawnshop— who becomes his symbolic son (replacing the lost David) and who is ultimately to be the agent of Sol's salvation.[3]

Sol Nazerman, however, is a peculiarly unsympathetic "priest" to his ragged flock, ministering to his customers with a ruthless detachment. Mrs. Harmon, a steady customer, knows that "the man truly was made of stone," although she seems to receive great satisfaction from bargaining with him, and even succeeds occasionally in getting an extra dollar. George Smith, a child molester who enjoys reading philosophical books, sometimes manages to engage Sol in conversation about them—his visits to the pawnshop are really only excuses to talk. But generally Sol spares no consideration for the feelings of his clientele; caring nothing for their loneliness, their sorrows, their stories or their tears, he merely evaluates their goods, states his offer and writes out a ticket—"The shop creaked with other people's sorrows; he abided" (p. 22). Surrounded by Hawthorne's "great chain of humanity," he remains coldly unconcerned.

While Sol appears to be a god/priest to his congregation of lost souls, he is not omnipotent even in his small sphere. His shop is owned by Albert Murillio, a racketeer who uses the pawnshop as a front for various illegal enterprises, among them prostitution. Murillio shares Nazerman's callous attitude, expressing no feeling for people, for the "scum" that his various businesses feed on. Significantly, only he is never intimidated by Sol, who seems fearful of him (a sign that Sol is still capable of redemption). In one scene of confrontation, Sol is dwarfed by Murillio: "Though he was a much shorter man than Sol, he now seemed very big, hung over the pawnbroker like some dangerous weight. His eyes were so close that Sol could see the icy lacing of his irises" (p. 121). The image of cold, sharp eyes links him with Nazerman, whose eyes were earlier described as "needles"; clearly, the gangster Murillio is only a larger projection of the pawnbroker's own merciless manner. Sol, however, who during the novel is beginning to awaken again to participation in life and a sense of his kinship with the people around him, decides eventually that he can no longer deal with Murillio because of his involvement in prostitution. His reasoning is clarified in one of the memory flashbacks, in which Sol is forced to relive the experience of having to watch his wife perform fellatio on a German guard. Later, when Murillio attempts to force Sol's cooperation in one of his deals by threatening him with a gun, Wallant draws the moral in detailing Sol's shocked response: "He should have remembered more faithfully that this was the real taste of life, that it was not confined to dreams" (p. 123). As past and present seem increasingly to converge, Sol gradually recognizes his own implication in the crimes of inhumanity, and he moves toward acknowledgment of the "real taste of life" that alone can release him from his tormenting dreams.

Nazerman must put up with the city's refuse during business hours, and his home life offers him little refuge from the pervasive ugliness. His family in Mount Vernon are grotesques of a different kind, deformed by affluence and by the obsessive desire to be middle class. Sol's relationship to them is summed up when he arrives home with only a weary sense that "there were obstacles between him and his bed."

Wallant portrays the family as a collection of unattractive stereotypes. Bertha, Sol's sister, is loud, showy and acquisitive, delighting in her family's Americanness ("You wouldn't even know they were Jews.") Her husband Selig is a pretentious intellectual who can't support his family and so depends on Sol for handouts. Their daughter Joan is a spoiled suburban teenager, who, like her father, enjoys showing off her clichéd opinions. Morton, the son, however, is an outcast—sullen and seemingly unmotivated, he is constantly criticized and harassed by his family ("Sometimes I'm ashamed for the neighbors," his mother says. "My own son walking around, acting and looking like a bum."). Sol secretly likes Morton (the only member of his family he can tolerate) and pities him because of the treatment he receives; at times he even defends his nephew and reproves his sister for constantly nagging the boy.

Besides his sister, Sol's only other link with the past is Tessie, widow of his closest friend Rubin. In addition to his own family, Sol helps to support her and her dying father-in-law, who lives in her apartment. Sol's only "social" activity consists in his visits to Tessie, with whom he talks, plays cards, and makes love. But none of this is done with feeling—". . . there was very little passion between them and nothing of real love or tenderness, but, rather, that immensely stronger force of desperation and mutual anguish" (p. 50)—it is only a dance of death.

Marilyn Birchfield, a social worker who tries to break through Nazerman's shell, bridges the gap between his personal and business worlds. When she introduces herself to him in the pawnshop, saying that she is new in the area and is seeking support for the youth center down the block, Sol tells her harshly that he is not interested in her talk but is willing to give her the "handout" she seeks. Shaken but undaunted, she accepts his money. Later, she tries again to befriend him; one day she brings sandwiches to the park and offers to share them with him. Sol rebuffs her, but she persists, telling him the story of her childhood and how she discovered loneliness; this only prompts Sol to ridicule her again, venting the bitterness of his superior suffering on her attempt at intimacy:

> "My dear Miss Birchfield, how touchingly naive you still are.
> . . . You discovered loneliness, you found that life was unjust
> and cruel. . . . There is this, my dear *sociologist*. People who
> have suffered in your little world may or may not become bitter,
> depending perhaps, on the state of their digestive system, or
> whether they were weaned too early in infancy. But wait, this
> you have not considered. There is a world so different in scale
> that its emotions bear no resemblance to yours; it has emotions
> so different in degree that they have become a different
> *species!*" (pp. 109–10)

One of the novel's most moving scenes occurs when Sol and Miss Birchfield, having at last reached some understanding, take a ferry ride together on the river. For once Sol is able to relax, to enjoy the peaceful moment and even Miss Birchfield's company. The symbolic function of the river is important in Wallant's fiction, representing the mystic qualities of life and death. Fish and the river function as instruments of rebirth in *The Human Season* and in *The Pawnbroker* as well. At the end of this novel, as he becomes reborn, Sol notes, ". . . the river . . . so vast in its total, never anything here and now, as it hurried slowly toward the obscurity of the salty ocean; so great so touching in its fleeting presence. The wetness dried on his cheeks and a great calm came over him" (p. 205). As Sol is ready to reunite himself with humanity, the river becomes, for him and for Wallant, a force that sums up the mystery of life itself.

The most important relationship in the novel, however, is that of Nazerman and his assistant Jesus Ortiz, for it is in the symbolic power of this association that the novel centers its thematic effect. As Nazerman's assistant and student, Ortiz admires his employer's intelligence and is fascinated by his air of mystery. Sol seems to have access to some secret knowledge that Ortiz would like to share: "Only the Pawnbroker, with his cryptic eyes, his huge secret body, seemed to have some sly key, some talisman of *knowing*." Ortiz is anxious to make his way in the world, to escape the Harlem street life, and he feels that Sol can teach him the business; he questions Sol about the testing of gold and the secrets of the Jew's success in business and religion. Sol's answers have a profound effect on him, motivating his actions and greatly influencing his thinking. Finally, it is Sol's bitter insistence that the only thing he values is money, that all people are "abominations" in his eyes, which disillusions his assistant and leads Ortiz to consider robbing the pawnshop.

Despite Sol's cold, irresponsible manner toward Ortiz, he is equally mystified by his assistant: "Sol frowned to cover the feeling of awe he always experienced when he first saw the brown-skinned youth in the morning" (p. 19); he tells Marilyn Birchfield, "I have a strange assistant, my Jesus Ortiz. I understand him as little as he understands me" (p. 111). The uneasy, unrealized father-son relationship between the two is reinforced and invested with thematic depth in the religious symbolism that unites them—the assistant's enigmatic charm

is described in terms that recall the popular representations of
Jesus Christ:

> Ortiz dazed him with the peculiar beauty of his smile again.
> There was something dangerous and wild on his smooth face, a
> look of guile and unpredictable curiosity; and yet, oddly, there
> was an unnerving quality of volatile innocence there, too. (p. 11)

At one point when Ortiz is questioning Sol, trying to fathom
the mystery of his employer's personality, he naively enquires
about the numbers tatooed on his arm (the concentration
camp identification code). "It's a secret society I belong to,"
Sol answers. "You could never belong. You have to be able to
walk on water" (p. 19). In light of Ortiz's symbolic role in the
novel, the line is even more heavily ironic than Nazerman
intends. Later, worried about Sol's puzzling change of
mood—he is beginning to emerge from his emotional
paralysis—Ortiz suddenly visualizes Sol in terms of Christ,
thus confirming the identification of father and son:

> And He was a Jew, too, just like the Pawnbroker; there's a laugh
> for you. He tried to imagine the Pawnbroker in a position like
> that, nailed up on a cross, the heavy, graceless body broken and
> naked, the great puffy face bent to one side . . . with the glasses
> on! He began to chuckle harshly. . . . (p.176)

The laugh is significant, for here, as in *The Children at the
Gate* and *The Tenants of Moonbloom*, Wallant uses it to signal
the achievement of significant insight and understanding.

Sol's emotional resurrection, slowly and painfully detailed,
is triggered by the approach of the anniversary of his family's
extermination. As his dreams impinge ever more closely upon
his conscious experience, the pain of the past begins gradually
to open him up to his life in the present. A significant moment
occurs when he recalls the death of his daughter Naomi:

> He was standing with his hands up to his cheeks, staring at the
> child's dead body twisted on a monstrous hook which pierced it

from behind and came out the breast. He began screaming, the screams of such unbearable size that the sensation was that of vomiting or giving birth. . . .

And then suddenly, there on the same childish body appeared another face . . . a young man's thin, sallow face—Morton! And then there appeared the lined, pathetically depraved face of George Smith. And then the face was that of Jesus Ortiz. (pp. 143–44)

Sol's sympathies are thus beginning to converge, his grief becoming more universalized as he learns to perceive the kinship in suffering that unites humanity in a struggle against the inevitable pain of existence. He still tries to squelch this vision, which yet brings him no relief, to hold on to his nihilism and his indifference, but the nightmares continue to intrude and leave him no peace.

The final searing memory is of his work in the camp crematoriums. It is significant that there he was burning the dead, for that is precisely what he must do in the present—exorcise the demonic images of the dead past that have so long paralyzed him. As if to signal his completion of this task and his readiness to re-enter life, his next memory is a pleasant one, of a family outing before the coming of the Nazis. Here Wallant's description captures the pastoral quality of the scene, in language quite different from the harsh, cold diction that characterizes the concentration camp sequences:

He walked up the gentle slope with the jar of milk and the bottle of white wine cold and wet from the brook where he had cooled them. Butterflies anticipated his route, swirling up from the high grass in palpitating clouds of color; there was the hot, peaceful din of insects all around, a drowsy twittering of sunweakened birds. (p. 177)

The Pawnbroker's actual redemption comes at the hands of Jesus Ortiz, who loses his own life in the attempt to save Sol's. Depressed and confused by Sol's cynical tirade about the meaninglessness of human life, Ortiz agrees to help his hoodlum friends rob the pawnshop, only insisting that there be no shooting. But when the gang members demand that Sol hand over his money, he refuses, for he sees death as an escape from his torment and so does not fear their threats. Ortiz, however, suddenly jumps in front of Nazerman in order to shield him, and is fatally wounded in the confusion. This "son's" sacrifice for the sake of his spiritual father is an incident of such symbolic and emotional power that Sol is suddenly transformed by it, at last shaken out of his lifeless apathy. Again, the moment of awareness is underscored with incongruous laughter:

> All his anesthetic numbness left him. He became terrified of the touch of air on the raw wounds. What was this great, agonizing sensitivity and what was it for? Good God, what was all this? Love? Could this be *love*? He began to laugh hysterically. . . . (p. 200)

His first significant action is to ask his nephew Morton to help him in the shop. "I need you, Morton," he says, thus adopting, this time deliberately and with unobstructed affection, a new surrogate son.

In a doctor's office Sol experiences his final vision, this one encompassing both past and future and promising his future involvement with the living rather than the dead:

> He walked over a strangely desolate and overgrown meadow with Tessie and Morton. They were silent and seemed indifferent to him, yet they kept pace with him, step for step. . . . A black uniformed figure came out of the nearest building. . . . He walked stiffly up to Sol and looked up at him with empty eye sockets; it was Murillio. Then he faced down to a slip of paper in his hand and he read:
> "Your dead are not buried here." (p. 203)

Earlier linked with Murillio by the cold, sharp eyes that suggested their shared insensitivity to the suffering around them, Sol is thus informed by the gangster's eyeless spector (Murillio is now dead) that his past does not belong in this time, this place. Sol's dead "are not buried here," and so his grief, all-consuming before, must give way to new life and new opportunities for love. Tessie and Morton, his new family, walk in the field where he last knew happiness with his old one. Motivated by this sense of renewal, Sol walks out of his tomb-like store and symbolically joins the streaming humanity in the streets (the river image recurs to suggest a baptismal immersion in the water of life): "So he was caught in the flow of them as he tried to find the wellspring of his own tears." Redeemed to feeling, he now accepts the burden of suffering and pain as part of living, "if not happily like a martyr, at least willingly like an heir." Finally, he decides to visit Tessie and help her to mourn the death of her father-in-law, whose passing marks the end of the chain of relationships that have kept the survivors tied to a deathly memory.

Wallant's novel is certainly a flawed work, for he does not always succeed in it in maintaining a balance between the realistic and the symbolic modes of his narrative: the religious symbolism is at times heavy-handed and melodramatic, while some purely practical developments, such as Sol's surprise at learning that the sinister Murillio has illegal business dealings, ring false. It seems that there is too much crowded into one story—too much extraneous characterization of Sol's customers, too much concentration on the clichéd family life in Mount Vernon, too much diversity and complexity of focus. On the other hand, Wallant's old-fashioned faith in human redemption is powerfully manifested in the figure of Sol Nazerman, whose reawakening from the horrors of holocaust seems to encompass the whole history of physical and mental suffering that galvanizes the modern sensibility. Through his talent in creating vivid characters, his command of dramatic episode, and his poetic manipulation of prose description and dialogue, Wallant manages to maintain in *The Pawnbroker* a strong, if occasionally uncontrolled, grip on the moral imagination. In the two novels that were to follow before his death—*The Children at the Gate* and *The Tenants of Moonbloom*—he would render the same allegorical vision more subtly, creating memorable expressions of modern man's potential for emotional and spiritual regeneration.

The film version of *The Pawnbroker* is a faithful adaptation, but more compressed than the original. Director Sidney Lumet and writers Morton Fine and David Friedkin have eliminated most of the episodes not directly related to the world of the pawnshop, instead focusing intently on the nightmare world that Nazerman (Rod Steiger) survived in the concentration camps and the one he has now created within himself.

Sol's customers, particularly George Smith and Marilyn Birchfield (Geraldine Fitzgerald), play much reduced roles in the film, developed as characters only insofar as they interact directly with Sol. Of the novel's central characters, only Ortiz (Jamie Sanchez) is shown to have a life outside the pawnshop. After working hours he is seen in the squalid apartment where he lives with his mother; it is established that he is an affectionate son, and his mother, who cannot speak English, clearly adores him. His relationship with Mabel Wheatly, a whore (not given a name in the film) who works for Murillio (renamed Roderiguez and transformed into a black man; he is played by Brock Peters), and with his street friends are also explored. Oddly enough, what the filmmakers fail to delineate fully is the important connection between Ortiz and Nazerman, the potential father-son identification that underlies the tension between them and highlights the symbolic dimension of their relationship. This omission ultimately proves to be the film's central weakness, for it leaves undefined the nature of the sacrifice of Jesus Ortiz, which is the culminating moment in the Pawnbroker's story.

The paring down of all the peripheral characters intensi-

The Pawnbroker: Sol Nazerman (Rod Steiger) cries over the body of his slain assistant, Jesus Ortiz (Jamie Sanchez), thereby rediscovering his buried emotional life.

fies the focus on the character of Nazerman, and Rod Steiger's bravura performance totally dominates the film. In his air of convulsive restraint, Wallant's haunting, grotesque, yet towering figure is brought vividly to life.

The film opens with a flashback, in slow motion, to an idyllic scene: Sol and his family are having a picnic, the children playing in a meadow. As they run into Sol's arms for a hug, the slow motion duplicates well the relaxed, lyrical tone which Wallant used to describe the scene (in the novel it comes near the end). Lumet's visual sequence slightly but significantly modifies Wallant's image, however, for in the novel when Sol's children approach him, they stop just out of reach: "Their faces all came closer; he would have liked to gather them all into him, to drink them, to breathe them. And then they stopped, every blade of grass froze, each of them was arrested in motion . . ." (p. 178); Lumet's version goes on to show Sol embracing the children, whirling them around. (This scene is to be repeated at the end of the film, its action at last completed: as Sol whirls his children, he suddenly sees Nazi soldiers coming to arrest him and his family.) Lumet's scenes thus emphasize more explicitly the shocking onset of disaster and Sol's sense of helplessness, the inability to save his family, which is the major cause of his profound guilt. Both scenes in the film end subjectively, representing Sol's limited point of view, turning the experience, which is developed conceptually in the novel, into an emotional moment of recognition which the film audience must share with Sol himself.

From the opening flashback, the film cuts abruptly to his sister's home in Long Island, where Sol lies resting on a lounge chair in the back yard, while various members of the family nag at him. The bright, harsh sunlight of the suburban scene, contrasting sharply with the hazy lighting of the pastoral memory sequence that preceded it, heightens the effect of oppressive vulgarity created by their banal, selfish chattering. After this obtrusive appearance, however, Sol's new family vanishes entirely from the story, not to figure further in either his suffering or his redemption. This opening scene of the contemporary narrative is thus stranded in isolation from the Harlem milieu that provides the setting for the rest of the action, and it seems rather pointless here—its irrelevance becomes even more noticeable upon subsequent viewings—since neither its characters nor its satiric flavor is to be encountered again in the film. As a glimpse of Sol's life beyond the pawnshop, it is too vaguely developed and too swiftly dropped to make any significant contribution to our understanding of the man's emotional situation. To be sure, the family sections in the novel are also poorly conceived, for Wallant chose to portray characters so crass and vapid that Sol's attitude toward them is easily excused. Neither the ostensible exploration of its protagonist's personal life nor the familiar exposé of middle-class values of assimilation contributes much to the novel's profound study of modern spiritual alienation. But in Wallant's version, the family scenes do at least serve to introduce Morton and to pave the way for Sol's calling him at the end; the filmmakers, however, have eliminated even this final, significant gesture, and so it remains unclear why they have bothered to introduce the family at all.

Next, Sol is seen driving to Harlem, parking his car, and opening his shop; the rest of the film, except for the flashbacks, takes place in the city, mostly in the pawnshop. Here Sol sits or stands behind an iron enclosure, the shadows of the bars that separate him from his customers reflected on his head and face, another explicit symbol of his emotional imprisonment.

The encounters between Sol and his customers are very similar to those in the novel, dialogue and character having been adapted faithfully. The filmmakers, though, have made Sol appear coarser, more alienated than his fictional counterpart—here he seems actually hostile to the people who come to the store. Wallant's Sol could manage some occasional tolerance, as in the case of Smith, with whom he would even discuss philosophy; in the film Sol coldly rebuffs all his attempts at conversation. With Marilyn Birchfield, too, he is continually rude in the film, displaying a savage, one-sided personality which makes him both less vulnerable and less easily sympathetic than Wallant's protagonist.

The scene between them on the ferry is eliminated, and in its place, is substituted a very awkwardly handled episode in which Sol visits Miss Birchfield in her apartment. Prior to this he has been walking the streets all night; the scene is full of glaring, out-of-focus lights and distorted angles, an overblown and ineffective illustration of Sol's spiritual crisis. The scene is plagued with weak dialogue, as she makes small talk and he explains woodenly that "everything was taken away from me and I did not die." Then comes the film's most embarrassing moment: from behind them, the camera shows Miss Birchfield stretching out her hand to him; they do not look at each other, and nothing happens; eventually she drops her arm and Sol leaves the apartment. The triteness of the gesture undercuts the attempted poignancy of the scene; Sol's inability to make any emotional contact has been long established, and this dumb dramatization only lessens its importance.

In an attempt to transfer Wallant's complex protagonist to the screen, to render explicit in dramatic terms the intensity of emotional effect, which the novelist painstakingly built up through symbolism, prose texturing, and internal perspective, the filmmakers have tended to reduce Sol to his essential, negative being. The corrosive isolation that remains his defining characteristic is yet again emphasized in the comments of Tessie's father-in-law, a character who is used in the film only to nag at Sol and thus to probe his spiritual wounds. When Sol first visits Tessie's house, the father-in-law (played by Lumet's father, Baruch Lumet) remarks sarcastically that Sol has come to "bring joy to a dead man's wife"; later he criticizes Sol for coming out of the camps "dead" and for being unable to feel joy or pain or love. The character thus functions as Sol's conscience, serving chiefly to underscore his spiritual problem. In the novel Selig (he is not named in the film) is presented in quite another way: he does not rant or criticize Sol, and even seems to like him. A very gentle man, he inspires some reciprocal feeling; when Sol speaks to him there is "a note of gentleness in his scorn." None of this tentative sympathy survives in the film, where the father-in-law's shrill censure operates only as a kind of voice from the grave, a mouthpiece for some rather tedious, and surely unnecessary, analysis of the protagonist's condition. Sol's state of death-in-life is being clearly and more dramatically developed in other ways.

One of Lumet's more effective methods for representing it involves some creative editing. In one sequence he intercuts parallel love scenes to emphasize Sol's lifelessness: Ortiz and his girl friend are shown making love (they are laughing, clutching, embracing, rolling about), their movement, vitality, and physical passion providing a vivid counterpoint to the alternate scenes in which Sol and Tessie glumly conclude his visit with a sexual encounter that seems more a matter of habit than of shared feeling. Sol rises slowly from a nap and removes his glasses as she unties her apron; then the camera, from above, dwells on Sol lying motionless on top of her, his hand seemingly independent of his body, clutching the pillow, while Tessie stares vacantly into space.

This technique of balancing parallel images is a central element of the film's structure, most consistently devoted to demonstrating the relationship of past and present. As film theorists explain, time becomes a spatial element on the screen, its passage indicated by a movement from point to point in space, rather than by any of the subtle transitional effects available to the writer. Lumet handles the temporal dislocation of Nazerman's consciousness very well in his use of the flashbacks, which explore the connections between his past and present experience. Whereas in the novel the flashback memories come to him in his dreams, not triggered by any specific current incidents, in the film Sol's past recurs to him in his waking state, prompted by occurrences that remind him of related or similar happenings in the past. The shifting time reference is graphically suggested by the sudden transference from Harlem to the concentration camp, accomplished by the substitution of some significant, parallel image for the one that is transfixing Sol in the present.

In the film, for example, he suddenly recalls his son's death in the cattle car while riding on a subway train, the memory activated by the sensation of vehicular motion. The film's rendering of this sequence is necessarily less detailed than Wallant's, reducing the deliberate sensationalism of the prose description to an acceptable, if still horrifying, visual experience of loss. The boy's grotesque death, vividly remembered in the novel as a sliding down into a "carpeting of feces" on the floor of the car, followed by the sound of him making "savage, empty, retches, vomiting and slipping around in the bottomless filth," is much too intense a physical experience to be depicted in the directness of film realism; it is replaced with a simple shot of the child slipping off Sol's shoulders, disappearing into the massed bodies of the other passengers. Still, the point is effectively made, as Sol's horrific memory of his helpless agony returns to torment him in even the most mundane situations.

This same strategy of restraint is again effective in another flashback sequence, this time involving the death of his friend. Here the savagery of Wallant's description is toned down by the enactment of only the end of the episode, as Rubin, pursued by guards, throws himself in desperation onto an electrically-charged fence; again, Lumet's editing skillfully masks the too graphic impact of the man's electrocution while retaining the full impression of Sol's retrospective anguish. This scene, too, has been inaugurated by Sol's current experience: the barking of a dog brings to mind the attack dogs of the camp; a kid climbing a playground fence to escape a gang suggests Rubin climbing the concentration camp fence; a young girl's attempt to pawn a ring becomes a ring being taken from the dead man's finger. Remembrance comes spasmodically, the images broken up into quick, two- or three-frame shots—obviously Sol doesn't want to remember and is struggling to block these flashes of memory from his mind, but eventually the horror overwhelms him and the entire sequence is presented. Like the other flashbacks, it is more brightly lighted, as if more compelling, more indelible in impression than the scenes of the present, which remain dark and shadowy, emphasizing the void which is Sol's life. (This bright/dark contrast becomes important again when Sol visits Roderiguez in his fashionably decorated apartment: the glaring whiteness of the modernistic furnishings there is reminiscent of the stark, harshly lighted concentration camp scenes, and this resemblance in setting links the past and present oppressors in a league against the gloomy, pawnshop world of their suffering victims.)

Lumet makes a narrative revision in the representation of one of the flashbacks, and this, as Joseph Lyons points out, significantly alters the meaning of the film.[4] When Ortiz's girl friend, desperate for money, bares her breast to Sol in order to arouse his interest in paying her for sex, he is suddenly reminded of his wife's forced prostitution in the prison camp. In the film, Sol watches in tortured pain while his wife performs fellatio on a soldier; here she never sees him, though in the novel she does:

> Sol began to moan. But just before tears could bring mercy to his eyes, he saw her recognize him. And from that hideously obscene position, pierced so vilely, she endured the zenith of her agony and was able to pass through it. Until finally she was able to award him the tears of forgiveness. But he was not worthy of her award and took the infinitely meaner triumph of blindness. . . . (p. 127)

The passage is significant, for Nazerman's isolation is confronted here with full force; in contrast with his wife, who finds the strength to forgive him, he is shown to be weak. His cutting himself off from his fellow man is here linked with mere survival, the implication being, in Lyons' words,

> . . . that he must isolate himself in order to survive, for recognition will bring self-destruction. While this retreat is understandable and humanizing, it makes him weak and shallow in contrast to his wife and the many there must have been like her. Yet in the film, both the wife's forgiveness and Nazerman's denial are ignored. She never sees him, and her attitude as she sits on her cot bespeaks only hopelessness and resignation. Because the communication between them is excluded, Nazerman's closure and abandonment is also excluded and he becomes nothing more than a martyr figure.[5]

The complex sense of desperation which makes Wallant's figure more rounded and, indeed, more noble is absent from the film. The novel projects a deeply wounded, yet sensitive man, capable of some varied response to his customers, his assistant, and Miss Birchfield. Lumet's, on the other hand, is a study in a single-minded, intense misanthropy; there is a touch of majesty in his isolation, as he towers above all the lesser people around him, yet all his well-articulated suffering seems to have produced no more than an all-consuming bitterness, self-confining and destructive.

The film effectively portrays this man's emotional dilemma, his absorption in the past, and the milieu of the pawnshop, but it ultimately fails to realize the novel's richness because of its vague development of the Nazerman-Ortiz relationship. In the novel the symbolic father-son relationship between them is carefully established, the young man's reverence for his boss and teacher involving a kind of religious awe; even Nazerman responds inexplicably to Ortiz, occasionally making awkward displays of affection toward him. In the film, however, Sol exhibits no feeling for his assistant except contempt. An attempt is made to indicate some kind of teacher-pupil arrangement, as Ortiz asks multiple, rapid questions and proposes to write down the Pawnbroker's lessons in a notebook, but no real communication ever develops between them. His questions seem devised rather to provoke from Sol the several set-piece monologues on Jewry, God, and money, in which Steiger seems to be addressing the camera instead of Ortiz, than to initiate any meaningful exchange of ideas and interest between the two characters. Finally, having created no convincing tension of relationship, the film can only deliver a symbolic sacrifice that, however immediately powerful in impression, must seem forced and arbitrary upon reflection.

Beyond this conceptual weakness, however, the film achieves a strong, emotional climax, as Lumet provides clear and compelling visual equivalents to Wallant's eloquent prose. As the wounded Ortiz crawls out of the shop to the street, the camera cuts to Sol's face and moves in close to discover the dawning awareness of his own involvement in this new pain. Slowly he walks through his shop and into the street, emerging from the tomb-like enclosure just as he is coming out of the spiritual prison within. Holding the bloody Ortiz in his arms, he cries a painful, voiceless cry, his face contorted and grotesque—the moment of utter agony is unforgettably portrayed in Steiger's tortured expression. Unlike his earlier cry of humiliation and frustration when taunted by Roderiguez, this is a cry of transcendent pain, an expression from a soul reawakening to anguished life, and thus it is linked to the blood on his hands.

Re-entering his shop, Sol stands behind the counter and stares at the paper spindle in front of him, as the faces of all the suffering people of his world swim before his eyes. Then slowly, deliberately, he pushes down on the metal spike, piercing his hand, forcing himself to feel the pain, in proof that he is now again alive. It is a bold, symbolic gesture; wholly original to the film, it provides an expressionistic sense of the intensity of the experience, which Wallant renders instead through description of Sol's internal state. The startling visual effect is entirely consonant with Wallant's dramatic vision, however, and it even seems likely that the filmmakers found their inspiration in the conclusion of another of his novels; at the end of *The Children at the Gate*, a spiritually-troubled character impales himself in desperation on the spiked hospital gate, which occurrence inspires the protagonist's resurrection of feeling:

> And a blade twitched into his heart, beginning that slow massive bleeding he would never be able to stop, no matter what else he might accomplish. He was surprised and puzzled as he walked with that mortal wound in him, for it occurred to him that, although the wound would be the death of him, it would be the life of him too.

Like the resurrection of the film's Sol Nazerman, who enacts its figurative language in literal terms, this passage projects the soul's rebirth within the traditional Christian image—thus sharing the crucifixion of Jesus Ortiz, the Pawnbroker experiences a miraculous spiritual renewal in the acceptance of human suffering. The film's last shot follows him out into the street once again, where he is quickly swallowed up in Wallant's "sea of humanity."

Steiger's brilliant performance and Lumet's re-creation of the Harlem low life and the pawnshop environment highlight the film. Such technical effects as parallel editing and contrapuntal lighting are used effectively to elucidate themes and suggest the symbolic resonances of Wallant's story. The film thus provides an unusually powerful emotional experience, although its intellectual statement is not entirely coherent. Grimly compelling, like the novel that inspired it, in its portrayal of modern man's spiritual crisis, the film *Pawnbroker* suffers from some thematic disunity that rather weakens the logic of its narrative, but cannot dispel the intensity of its dramatic vision.

NOTES

Chapter 1

[1] I am indebted to the following sources for biographical information on Cahan. Abraham Cahan, *The Education of Abraham Cahan*, trans. Leon Stein, Abraham P. Conan, and Lynn Davison (Philadelphia: Jewish Publication Society, 1969). This is a translation of the first two volumes of *Bleter fun Mein Leben* (Pages from My Life), Cahan's five volume autobiography (New York: The Forward Association, 1926–1931). The forthcoming volume will complete the translation. Ronald Sanders, *The Downtown Jews* (New York: Harper and Row, 1969). Jules Chametzky, *From the Ghetto: The Fiction of Abraham Cahan* (Amherst: The University of Massachusetts Press, 1977).

[2] Quoted in Chametzky, pp. 68–69.

[3] Abraham Cahan, *The Rise of David Levinsky* (1917; rpt. New York: Harper and Row, 1966), p. 530.

[4] Abraham Cahan, *Yekl: A Tale of the New York Ghetto* (1896; rpt. New York: Dover Publishing Co., 1970), p. 5. All further references to the novel are cited in the text and refer to this edition.

[5] Chametzky, p. 64.

[6] One of the joys of the film is the consistently excellent acting. Carol Kane as Gitel and Stephen Keats as Jake are both superb. As are Mel Howard (Bernstein), Doris Roberts (Mrs. Kavarsky), and Dorrie Kavanaugh (Mamie).

[7] Raymond Durgnat, *Films and Feelings* (1967; rpt. Cambridge: The M.I.T. Press, 1971), p. 39.

Chapter 2

[1] Isaac F. Marcossen, *David Graham Phillips: His Life and Times* (New York: Dodd, Mead and Co., 1932), p. 83. I am also indebted to Abe C. Ravitz, *David Graham Phillips* (New York: Twayne Publishers, 1966) and Louis Filler, *Voice of Democracy: A Critical Biography of David Graham Phillips* (University Park: Pennsylvania State Univ. Press, 1978) for the biographical information used in this chapter.

[2] Quoted in Ravitz, p. 83.

[3] Marcossen, p. 282.

[4] David Graham Phillips, *Susan Lenox: Her Fall and Rise* (1917; rpt. New York: Popular Library, 1978), p. 117. All further references are cited in the text and refer to this edition.

[5] Elizabeth Janeway, "Afterword" to *Susan Lenox* (Carbondale: Southern Illinois Univ. Press, 1977), p. xiii.

[6] Andrew Bergman, *We're in the Money* (1971; rpt. New York: Harper & Row, 1972), p. 51.

[7]*Ibid.*

[8]Bergman, p. 52.

[9]Lyn Tornabene, *Long Live the King: A Biography of Clark Gable* (1976; rpt. New York: Pocket Books, 1978), p. 138.

[10]John Douglas Eames, *The MGM Story* (New York: Crown Publishers, 1976), p. 74. Lyn Tornabene in her biography of Gable writes that 22 writers worked on the script. Official credit went to Wanda Tuchock, Zelda Sears, and Leon Gordon.

[11]Considering the nature of Phillips' material, the film, at least, would have been better off at Warner Bros., a studio which dealt with social issues better than its wealthier and more glamorous competitors.

Chapter 3

[1]Peter Brunette and Gerald Peary, "Tough Guy: James M. Cain Interviewed," *Film Comment,* May–June 1976, p. 57.

[2]*Ibid.*

[3]David Madden, "James M. Cain and the Movies of the Thirties and Forties," *Film Heritage,* II, Summer 1967, p. 19.

[4]James M. Cain, preface, *The Butterfly* (1947; rpt. New York: Dell Publishing Co., 1964), p. 10.

[5]Edmund Wilson, "The Boys in the Back Room" in *Classics and Commercials* (1950; rpt. New York: Knopf, 1962), pp. 20–21.

[6]Richard Lehan, *A Dangerous Crossing* (Carbondale: Southern Illinois Univ. Press, 1973), p. 62.

[7]W. M. Frohock, *The Novel of Violence in America* (1950; rpt. Boston: The Beacon Press, 1964).

[8]*Ibid.,* p. 13.

[9]Albert Van Nostrand, *The Denatured Novel* (1960; rpt. Indianapolis: Bobbs-Merrill, 1962), pp. 126–132.

[10]Wilson, p. 22.

[11]David Madden, *James M. Cain* (New York: Twayne Publishers, 1970).

[12]Roy Hoopes, "An Appreciation of James M. Cain," *The New Republic,* 22 July 1978, p. 25.

[13]James M. Cain, *The Postman Always Rings Twice* in *Three Novels by James M. Cain* (New York: Bantam Books, 1973), p. 24. All further references to the novel are cited in the text and refer to this edition.

[14]Frohock, p. 20.

[15]Madden, *James M. Cain,* p. 176.

[16]Madden, *James M. Cain,* p. 159.

[17]David Madden, "Cain's *The Postman Always Rings Twice* and Camus' *L'Etranger,*" *Papers on Language and Literature,* V (Fall 1970), p. 419.

[18]Raymond Durgnat, "The Family Tree of Film Noir," *Film Comment* (November–December 1974), pp. 6–7.

[19]Stephen Farber, "Violence and the Bitch Goddess," *Film Comment* (November–December 1974), p. 9.

[20]Richard Dyer, "Lana: Four Films of Lana Turner," *Movie*, 25, pp. 38–39.

[21]*Ibid.*, p. 38.

[22]Joyce Carol Oates, "Man Under Sentence of Death: The Novels of James M. Cain," in *Tough Guy Writers of the Thirties*, ed. David Madden (Carbondale: Southern Illinois Univ. Press, 1968), p. 113.

[23]*Ibid.*, p. 124.

Chapter 4

[1]John Thomas Sturak's unpublished doctoral dissertation, "The Life and Writings of Horace McCoy, 1897–1955" is to date the only substantial treatment of McCoy's work yet written.

[2]Allene S. Talmey, "Paris Quick Notes/About Sartre, Gide, Cocteau, Politics/The Theatre, and Inflation," *Vogue*, 109 (January 15, 1947), 92.

[3]Robert Bourne Linscott, "On the Books," *New York Herald Tribune Book Review*, February 9, 1947.

[4]Paul S. Nathan, "Books Into Films," *Publisher's Weekly*, 153 (June 5, 1948), 2391.

[5]Quoted in John Thomas Sturak, "The Life and Writings of Horace McCoy, 1897–1955," Dissertation, University of California, Los Angeles, 1966, pp. 265–69.

[6]*Ibid.*, p. 260.

[7]*Ibid.*, p. 265.

[8]*Ibid.*, p. ix.

[9]*Ibid.*, pp. 265–69.

[10]Horace McCoy, *They Shoot Horses, Don't They?* (1935; rpt. New York: Avon, 1970), p. 125. All further references to the novel are cited in the text and refer to the Avon edition.

[11]Sturak, pp. 278–79.

[12]*Ibid.*, p. 281. This can also be found in Thomas Sturak, "Horace McCoy's Objective Lyricism" in *Tough Guy Writers of the Thirties*, ed. David Madden (Carbondale: Southern Illinois Univ. Press, 1968).

[13]*Ibid.*, p. 291.

[14]John Simon, *Movies Into Film* (1971; rpt. New York: Dell Publishing Co., 1972), p. 86. Also in Joseph Morgenstern and Stefan Kanfer, eds., *Film 69/70* (New York: Simon & Schuster, 1970), p. 98.

[15]Sidney Pollack, "Forward to the Screenplay," in Horace McCoy, *They Shoot Horses, Don't They?* (New York: Avon, 1970), p. 134.

[16]In the published version of the screenplay Robert E. Thompson is given full credit. Poe's name is not mentioned.

[17]Robert E. Thompson, *They Shoot Horses, Don't They?: A Screenplay* in Horace McCoy, *They Shoot Horses, Don't They?* (New York: Avon, 1970), pp. 148–49. All further references to the screenplay are cited in the text and refer to this edition.

[18]Nathanael West, *Miss Lonelyhearts & The Day of the Locust* (1939; rpt. New York: New Directions, 1969), pp. 177–78.

[19]Simon, pp. 84–85.

[20]In James Poe's original script Rocky displays no compassionate side. For Poe's story of how the producers, director, et al., "ruined" his film, see Michael Dempsey, "Trials and Traumas: James Poe" in *The Hollywood Screenwriters* (New York: Avon, 1972), pp. 181–204.

Chapter 5

[1]Brandon French, "Lost at Sea," in *The Classic American Novel and the Movies*, ed. Gerald Peary and Roger Shatzkin (New York: Frederick Ungar Publishing Co., 1977), p. 53.

[2]Judy Stone, *The Mystery of B. Traven* (California: William Kaufmann Inc., 1977), p. 47.

[3]Quoted in Donald O. Chankin, *Anonymity and Death: The Fiction of B. Traven* (University Park: The Pennsylvania State Univ. Press, 1975), pp. 5–6.

[4]Michael Baumann, *B. Traven: An Introduction* (Albuquerque: Univ. of New Mexico Press, 1976), p. 17. I am indebted to Baumann as well as Chankin and Stone for the biographical information that appears in this chapter.

[5]*Ibid.*, p. 18.

[6]*Ibid.*, p. 27.

[7]Chankin, pp. 304. Also in Stone, pp. 73–74.

[8]Stone, p. 83.

[9]B. Traven, *The Treasure of the Sierra Madre* (1935; rpt. New York: New American Library, 1968), pp. 54–55. All further references to the novel are cited in the text and refer to this edition.

[10]Hannah Arendt, *Origins of Totalitarianism* (New York: Harcourt, Brace Jovanovich, 1951).

[11]See Thomas A. Kirby, "The Pardoner's Tale and The Treasure of the Sierra Madre," *Modern Language Notes*, 66 (1951):269–270.

[12]Ibid.

[13]Baumann, p. 81.

[14]James Agee, *Agee on Film* (Boston: Beacon Press, 1968), p. 290.

[15]Stuart Kaminsky, *John Huston: Maker of Magic* (Boston: Houghton Mifflin Co., 1978), p. 54.

Chapter 6

[1]In this context it is interesting to note that Kubrick has often relied on the works of distinguished authors as the bases of his films, having adapted for the screen Vladimir Nabokov's *Lolita*, Anthony Burgess' *A Clockwork Orange*, Arthur Clarke's *2001: A Space Odyssey*, and William Makepeace Thackeray's *Barry Lyndon*.

[2]Only Norman Kagen in *The Cinema of Stanley Kubrick* (1972; rpt. New York: Grove Press, 1975) mentions Cobb and then only briefly.

³The above biographical information can be found in The Book-of-the-Month Club's Newsletter on *Paths of Glory,* June 1935.

⁴Stanley Cooperman, *World War I and the American Novel* (Baltimore: Johns Hopkins Univ. Press, 1967), p. 61.

⁵*Ibid.,* p. 62.

⁶*Ibid.,* p. 63.

⁷This appears in Cobb's own note at the end of the novel.

⁸Warren Eyster, "Afterword" to the reprint of *Paths of Glory* (New York: Avon, 1973), p. 218. This essay also appears in David Madden, ed., *Rediscoveries* (New York: Crown Publishers, 1971), pp. 135–46.

⁹*Paths of Glory* was in Faulkner's library. See Joseph Blotner, *Faulkner: A Biography* (New York: Random House, 1974), pp. 903, 1500.

¹⁰*New York Times Book Review,* June 2, 1935, p. 1.

¹¹Humphrey Cobb, *Paths of Glory* (1935; rpt. New York: Avon, 1973), pp. 104–5. All further references to the novel are cited in the text and refer to this edition.

¹²Eyster, p. 220.

Chapter 7

¹Stanley Young, rev. of *Homage to Blenholt,* in *The New York Times,* Feb. 23, 1936, p. 6.

²Irving Howe, "Daniel Fuchs: Escape From Williamsburg," *Commentary* (July 1948), p. 31.

³Daniel Fuchs, *Low Company,* in *3 Novels by Daniel Fuchs* (New York: Basic Books, 1961), p. 28. The paperback edition entitled *The Williamsburg Trilogy* (New York: Avon, 1972) uses the same pagination as does the original edition (New York: Vanguard, 1937).

⁴Randall Reid, *The Fiction of Nathanael West* (Chicago: Univ. of Chicago Press, 1971), p. 144.

⁵*Ibid.,* p. 145.

⁶Robert Warshow, *The Immediate Experience* (New York: Atheneum, 1970), p. 133.

⁷Warshow, p. 133.

⁸The part was originally offered to Edward G. Robinson, who turned it down. Ernest Borgnine was also offered the part, but he didn't like it either. (Letter from Fuchs to G. Miller, June 1, 1976)

⁹George Bluestone, *Novels into Film* (Berkeley: University of California Press, 1971).

¹⁰Lester Asheim in his Ph.D. thesis, *From Book to Film* (University of Chicago, 1949), points out that in a sample of twenty-four film adaptations, seventeen increased the love interest. (Cited in Bluestone)

¹¹Colin McArthur, *Underworld U.S.A.* (New York: The Viking Press, 1972), p. 46.

Chapter 8

¹The novel's symbolic structure, especially the notion of the store as a tomb and the employer/assistant relationship, is very similar to Bernard Malamud's use of the store and the relationship between Morris Bober and Frank Alpine in *The Assistant*.

²Edward Lewis Wallant, *The Pawnbroker* (1961; rpt. New York: Macfadden-Bartell Books, 1965), p. 108. All further references to the novel are cited in the text and refer to this edition.

³For a more detailed discussion of Wallant's use of names in *The Pawnbroker*, see William V. Davis, "Learning to Walk on Water: Edward Lewis Wallant's *The Pawnbroker*," *The Literary Review*, 17 (Winter 1973–74), pp. 149–165.

⁴Joseph Lyons, "*The Pawnbroker:* Flashback in the Novel and Film," *Western Humanities Review*, XX (1966) 247.

⁵*Ibid.*, p. 248.

FILM CREDITS

(**Code: D** = Director; **Sc** = Screenwriter; **Ph** = Director of Photography; **M** = Music; **P** = Producer)

Hester Street (1975)

D: Joan Micklin Silver. **Sc:** Joan Micklin Silver. **Ph:** Kenneth Van Sickle. **M:** William Bolcom. **P:** Raphael D. Silver/Midwest Film Productions.

Cast: Stephen Keats (*Jake*), Carol Kane (*Gitel*), Mel Howard (*Bernstein*), Dorrie Kavanaugh (Mamie), Doris Roberts (Mrs. Kavarsky), Paul Freedman (*Joey*), Lauren Frost (*Fanny*), Zvee Scooler (*Rabbi*).

Running Time: 92 minutes.

Susan Lenox (1931)

D: Robert Z. Leonard. **Sc:** Wanda Tuchock, Zelda Sears & Leon Gordon. **P:** MGM.

Cast: Greta Garbo (Susan Lenox), Clark Gable (Rodney), Jean Hersholt (Ohlin), John Miljan (Burlingham), Alan Hale (Mondstrum), Hale Hamilton (Mike Kelly), Ian Keith (Robert Lane).

Running Time: 75 minutes.

The Postman Always Rings Twice (1946)

D: Tay Garnett. **Sc:** Harry Ruskin & Niven Busch. **Ph:** Sidney Wagner. **P:** Carey Wilson/MGM.

Cast: Lana Turner (*Cora Smith*), John Garfield (*Frank Chambers*), Cecil Kellaway (*Nick Smith*), Hume Cronyn (*Arthur Keats*), Leon Ames (*Kyle Sackett*), Audrey Totter (*Madge Garland*).

Running Time: 113 minutes.

They Shoot Horses, Don't They? (1969)

D: Sydney Pollack. **Sc:** Robert E. Thompson & James Poe. **Ph:** Philip Lathrop. **M:** John Green. **P:** Irwin Winkler, Robert Chartoff/ABC.

Cast: Jane Fonda (*Gloria Beatty*), Michael Sarrazin (*Robert Syverten*), Susannah York (*Alice*), Gig Young (*Rocky*), Red Buttons (*Sailor*), Bonnie Bedelia (*Ruby*), Bruce Dern (*James*), Robert Conrad (*Rollo*).

Running Time: 121 minutes.

The Treasure of the Sierra Madre (1948)

D: John Huston. **Sc:** John Huston. **Ph:** Ted McCord. **M:** Max Steiner. **P:** Henry Blanke/Warner Bros.

Cast: Humphrey Bogart (*Dobbs*), Walter Huston (*Howard*), Tim Holt (*Curtin*), Bruce Bennett (*Cody*), Barton MacLane (*McCormick*), Alfonso Bedoya (*Gold Hat*), Robert Blake (*Mexican boy*).

Running Time: 126 minutes.

Paths of Glory (1957)

D: Stanley Kubrick. **Sc:** Calder Willingham & Jim Thompson. **Ph:** George Krause. **M:** Gerald Fried. **P:** James B. Harris/United Artists.

Cast: Kirk Douglas (*Colonel Dax*), Ralph Meeker (*Paris*), Adolphe Menjou (*Broulard*), George Macready (*Mireau*), Wayne Morris (*Roget*), Richard Anderson (*Saint-Auban*), Joseph Turkel (*Arnaud*), Timothy Carey (*Ferol*), Bert Freed (*Boulanger*).

Running Time: 86 minutes.

The Gangster (1947)

D: Gordon Wiles. **Sc:** Daniel Fuchs. **Ph:** Paul Ivano. **M:** Louis Gruenberg. **P:** Maurice & Frank King/Allied Artists.

Cast: Barry Sullivan (*Shubunka*), Belita (*Nancy*), Joan Lorring (*Dorothy*), Akim Tamiroff (*Jamey*), Henry Morgan (*Shorty*), John Ireland (*Karty*), Sheldon Leonard (*Cornell*), Fifi D'Orsay (*Mrs. Ostraleng*).

Running Time: 84 minutes.

The Pawnbroker (1964)

D: Sidney Lumet. **Sc:** David Friedkin & Morton Fine. **Ph:** Boris Kaufman. **M:** Quincy Jones. **P:** Philip Langner & Robert H. Lewis/Landau Co.

Cast: Rod Steiger (*Sol Nazerman*), Geraldine Fitzgerald (*Marilyn Birchfield*), Brock Peters (*Roderiguez*), Jaime Sanchez (*Jesus Oritz*), Thelma Oliver (*Ortiz' Girl*), Marketa Kimbrell (*Tessie*), Raymond St. Jacques (*Tangee*), Charles Dierkop (*Robinson*), Juano Hernandez (*Mr. Smith*).

Running Time: 114 minutes.

FILM RENTAL SOURCES

Hester Street
Cinema 5
595 Madison Ave.
New York, N.Y. 10022
(212) 421-5555

They Shoot Horses, Don't They?
The Postman Always Rings Twice
Susan Lenox: Her Fall and Rise
Films Inc.
440 Park Ave. South
New York, N.Y. 10016
(212) 889-7910

476 Plasamour Dr. N.E.
Atlanta, GA 30324
(404) 873-5101

1144 Wilmette Ave.
Wilmette, IL 60091
(312) 256-6600

5625 Hollywood Blvd.
Hollywood, CA 90028
(213) 466-5481

The Gangster
Hurlock Cine-World

13 Arcadia Rd.
Old Greenwich, CT 06870
(203) 637-4139

Paths of Glory
The Treasure of the Sierra Madre
United Artists 16
729 Seventh Avenue
New York, N.Y. 10019
(212) 575-4715

The Pawnbroker
Macmillan/Audio Brandon
34 MacQueen Parkway So.
Mount Vernon, N.Y. 10550
(914) 664-5051

1619 North Cherokee
Los Angeles, CA 94611
(415) 658-9890

8400 Brookfield Ave.
Brookfield, IL 60513
(312) 485-3925

Also offices in Buffalo, NY,
Canton, OH, Denver, CO, and
Minneapolis, MN

SELECTED BIBLIOGRAPHY

Abraham Cahan

Primary (Works in English)

Yekl: A Tale of the New York Ghetto. D. Appleton & Co., 1896.
The Imported Bridegroom and Other Stories of the New York Ghetto. New York: Houghton Mifflin & Co., 1898.
The White Terror and the Red: A Novel of Revolutionary Russia. New York: A. S. Barnes & Co., 1905.
The Rise of David Levinsky. New York: Harpers, 1917.

Secondary

Chametzky, Jules. *From the Ghetto: The Fiction of Abraham Cahan.* Amherst: The Univ. of Massachusetts Press, 1977.
Hapgood, Hutchins. *The Spirit of the Ghetto.* New York: Funk and Wagnalls, 1902. Reprint, Cambridge: Harvard Univ. Press, 1967.
Rosenfeld, Isaac. "America, Land of the Sad Millionaire," *Commentary,* 14 (August 1952), pp. 131–135.
Sanders, Ronald. *The Downtown Jews: Portraits of an Immigrant Generation.* New York: Harper & Row, 1969.
Stein, Leon, Abraham P. Conan and Lynn Davison, trans. *The Education of Abraham Cahan.* Philadelphia: Jewish Publication Society of America, 1969.

James M. Cain

Primary

Our Government. New York: Knopf, 1930.
The Postman Always Rings Twice. New York: Knopf, 1934.
Serenade. New York: Knopf, 1937.
Mildred Pierce. New York: Knopf, 1941.
Love's Lovely Counterfeit. New York: Knopf, 1942.
Three of a Kind. New York: Knopf, 1943. (Contains *Career in C. Major, The Embezzler,* and *Double Indemnity*)
Past All Dishonor. New York: Knopf, 1946.
Sinful Woman. New York: Avon, 1947.
The Butterfly. New York: Knopf, 1947.
The Moth. New York: Knopf, 1948.
Jealous Woman. New York: Avon, 1950.
The Root of His Evil. New York: Avon, 1951.
Galatea. New York: Knopf, 1953.
Mignon. New York: The Dial Press, 1962.
The Magician's Wife. New York: The Dial Press, 1965.
Rainbow's End. New York: Mason/Charter, 1975.

Secondary

Madden, David. "James M. Cain's *The Postman Always Rings Twice* and Albert Camus's *L'Étranger.*" *Papers on Language and Literature*, V (Fall 1970).

————. *James M. Cain*. New York: Twayne Publishers, 1970.

Reck, Tom S. "J. M. Cain's Los Angeles Novels." *Colorado Quarterly*, 22 (Winter 1974).

Humphry Cobb

Primary

Paths of Glory. New York: Viking, 1935.
"None But the Brave." *Collier's*, Oct. 29–Dec. 3, 1938.

Secondary

Eyster, Warren. "Humphry Cobb's *Paths of Glory.*" In *Rediscoveries*, ed., David Madden. New York: Crown Publishers, 1971.

Daniel Fuchs

Primary

Summer in Williamsburg. New York: Vanguard, 1934.
Homage to Blenholt. New York: Vanguard, 1936.
Low Company. New York: Vanguard, 1937.
Stories, with Jean Stafford, William Maxwell, John Cheever. New York: Farrar, Straus & Cudahy, 1956.
3 Novels by Daniel Fuchs. (Includes *Summer in Williamsburg, Homage to Blenholt*, and *Low Company*) New York: Basic Books, 1961.
West of the Rockies. New York: Knopf, 1971.
The Apathetic Bookie Joint. New York: Methuen, 1979.

Secondary

Howe, Irving. "Daniel Fuchs: Escape from Williamsburg," *Commentary*, 6 (July 1948), pp. 29–34.

————. "Daniel Fuchs' Williamsburg Trilogy: A Cigarette and a Window." In *Proletarian Writers of the Thirties*, ed., David Madden. Carbondale: Southern Illinois Univ. Press, 1968.

Miller, Gabriel. "Screenwriter Daniel Fuchs: A Creed Grows in Brooklyn." *Los Angeles Times Book Review* (April 17, 1977), p. 3.

————. *Daniel Fuchs*. Boston: G. K. Hall & Co., 1979.

Horace McCoy

Primary

They Shoot Horses, Don't They? New York: Simon & Schuster, 1935.
No Pockets in a Shroud. London: Barker, 1937.

I Should Have Stayed Home. New York: Knopf, 1938.
Kiss Tomorrow Good-Bye. New York: Random House, 1948.
Scalpel. New York: Appleton-Century-Crofts, 1952.

Secondary

Richmond, Lee J. "A Time to Mourn and a Time to Dance: Horace McCoy's *They Shoot Horses, Don't They?*" *Twentieth Century Literature,* 2 (April 1971), pp. 91–100.
Sturak, John Thomas. "The Life and Writings of Horace McCoy, 1897–1955." Diss., Univ. of California, Los Angeles, 1966.
Sturak, John Thomas. "Horace McCoy's Objective Lyricism." In *Tough Guy Writers of the Thirties,* ed. David Madden. Carbondale: Southern Illinois Univ. Press, 1968.

David Graham Phillips

Primary

The Great God Success: A Novel. New York: Frederick A. Stokes Company, 1901.
Her Serene Highness: A Novel. New York & London: Harper & Brothers, 1902.
A Woman Ventures: A Novel. New York: Frederick A. Stokes Company, 1902.
Golden Fleece: The American Adventures of a Fortune Hunting Earl. New York: McClure, Phillips & Company, 1903.
The Master-Rogue: The Confessions of a Croesus. New York: McClure, Phillips & Company, 1903.
The Cost. Indianapolis: The Bobbs-Merrill Company, 1904.
The Mother-Light. New York: D. Appleton & Company, 1905. Published anonymously.
The Plum Tree. Indianapolis: The Bobbs-Merrill Company, 1905.
The Reign of Gilt. New York: James Pott & Company, 1905. Collected essays.
The Social Secretary. Indianapolis: The Bobbs-Merrill Company, 1905.
The Deluge. Indianapolis: The Bobbs-Merrill Company, 1905.
The Fortune Hunter. Indianapolis: The Bobbs-Merrill Company, 1906.
The Treason of the Senate. Stanford, California: Academic Reprints, n.d. 1954. Originally published *Cosmopolitan* (March–November, 1906).
The Second Generation. New York: D. Appleton & Company, 1907.
Light-Fingered Gentry. New York: D. Appleton & Company, 1907.
Old Wives for New: A Novel. New York: D. Appleton & Company, 1908.
The Worth of a Woman: A Play. New York: D. Appleton & Company, 1908.
The Fashionable Adventures of Joshua Craig: A Novel. New York: D. Appleton & Company, 1909.
The Hungry Heart: A Novel. New York & London: D. Appleton & Company, 1909.

White Magic: A Novel. New York & London: D. Appleton & Company, 1910.

The Husband's Story: A Novel. New York & London: D. Appleton & Company, 1910.

The Grain of Dust: A Novel. New York & London: D. Appleton & Company, 1911.

The Conflict: A Novel. New York & London: D. Appleton & Company, 1911.

The Price She Paid: A Novel. New York & London: D. Appleton & Company, 1912.

George Helm. New York & London: D. Appleton & Company, 1912.

Degarmo's Wife and Other Stories. New York & London: D. Appleton & Company, 1913.

Susan Lenox: Her Fall and Rise. New York & London: D. Appleton & Company, 1917. Two volumes.

Secondary

Filler, Louis. *Voice of Democracy: A Critical Biography of David Graham Phillips: Journalist, Novelist, Progressive.* University Park: The Pennsylvania State Univ. Press, 1978.

Marcossen, Isaac F. *David Graham Phillips: His Life and Times.* New York: Dodd, Mead & Co., 1932.

Ravitz, Abe C. *David Graham Phillips.* New York: Twayne Publishers, 1966.

B. Traven

Primary (*works in English in the order in which they appeared in the U.S.*)

The Death Ship. New York: Knopf, 1934.

――――. Translated by Erich Sutton. London: Chatto & Windus, 1934.

The Treasure of the Sierra Madre. New York: Knopf, 1935.

――――. Translated by Basil Creighton. London: Chatto & Windus, 1934.

The Bridge in the Jungle. New York: Knopf, 1938.

――――. London: Cape, 1940.

The Rebellion of the Hanged. New York: Knopf, 1952.

――――. Translated by Charles Duff. London: Robert Hale, 1952.

March to Monteira. New York: Dell, 1964. Originally published as *March to Caobaliand.* London: Hale, 1961.

The White Rose. London: Hale, 1965.

The Night Visitor and Other Stories. New York: Hill & Wang, 1966.

――――. London: Cassel, 1967.

Creation of the Sun and Moon. New York: Hill & Wang, 1968.

――――. London: Muller, 1971.

The Cotton Pickers. New York: Hill & Wang, 1969.

――――. Translated by Elanor Brocket. London: Robert Hale, 1956.

The Carreta. New York: Hill & Wang, 1970.

_____. Translated by Basil Creighton. London: Chatto & Windus, 1968.
Government. New York: Hill & Wang, 1971.
_____. Translated by Basil Creighton. London: Chatto & Windus, 1935.
General from the Jungle. Translated by Desmond Vesey. New York: Hill & Wang, 1922.
_____. Translated by Desmond I. Vesey. London: Robert Hale, 1954.
The Kidnapped Saint and Other Stories. Edited by Rosa Elena Lujan & Mina C. & H. Arthur Klein. New York: Lawrence Hill, 1975.

Secondary

Bauman, Michael L. *B. Traven: An Introduction.* Albuquerque: Univ. of New Mexico Press, 1976.
Chankin, Donald O. *Anonymity and Death: The Fiction of B. Traven.* University Park: The Pennsylvania State Univ. Press, 1975.
Stone, Judy. *The Mystery of B. Traven.* California: William Kaufmann, Inc., 1977.

Edward Lewis Wallant

Primary

The Human Season. New York: Harcourt, Brace & World, 1960.
The Pawnbroker. New York: Harcourt, Brace & World, 1961.
The Tenants of Moonbloom. New York: Harcourt, Brace & World, 1963.
The Children at the Gate. New York: Harcourt, Brace & World, 1964.

Secondary

Angle, James. "Edward Lewis Wallant's Trinity of Survival." *Kansas Quarterly,* 7 (Fall 1975), pp. 106–18.
Baumbach, Jonathan. *The Landscape of Nightmare: Studies in the Contemporary American Novel.* New York: New York Univ. Press, 1965.
Davis, William V. "Learning to Walk on Water: Edward Lewis Wallant's *The Pawnbroker.*" *The Literary Review,* 17 (Winter 1973–74), pp. 149–165.
Hoyt, Charles A., ed. *Minor American Novelists.* Carbondale: Southern Illinois Univ. Press, 1970.
Schulz, Max F. *Radical Sophistication: Studies in Contemporary Jewish/ American Novelists.* Athens: Ohio Univ. Press, 1969.
Stanford, Raney. "The Novels of Edward Wallant." *Colorado Quarterly,* XVII, 1969.

INDEX